PRAISE FOR

Woven as One

"Linda was my second mother, and I was her fourth son. Her youngest son, Alex, and I have been best friends since we were four years old, and the Waddell home was my second home and hangout whether it was in Richmond, Norfolk, or the beach. *Woven As One* is an amazing story about her shared love with Bill, her family, her friends, and her dogs and her ability to navigate and weather through chaos. It is a love story made of everyday things, well worth knowing and emulating."

—Jon Baliles, former Richmond city councilman, now author and podcaster

"This book moved me in a way few do. It speaks from the heart of someone who has known the quiet miracle of lifelong love—and the devastation of loss. As a therapist who sits daily with the ache of grief and the beauty of human connection, I found these pages to be both humbling and healing. With breathtaking honesty, it reminds us that love—fully given and fully received—is life's greatest gift. And though its absence can hollow us, its presence, even in memory, continues to shape and hold us. This is not just a book about loss. It is a love letter to presence, to partnership, and to the kind of love that leaves us forever changed."

—Jenny Pfeiffer, licensed professional counselor, certified life coach

"Waddell's raw honesty about love's deepest joys and most profound losses creates an unforgettable portrait of a couple whose chemistry burned bright for fifty-eight years of marriage. From belly dancing to owning a racetrack, and from skinny dipping to traveling the world, Bill and Linda's adventures are an inspiration to live more boldly. This is more than a love story; it's a celebration of a life lived fully alongside a soulmate and a poignant reminder that true love transcends even death."

—Meghan Davis Hill, author of *The Continuum of Change*

"Many of us have had priceless relationships with our spouses. Few of us, though, have the patience, power of recall, sense of humor, and writing skill to pen a work as interesting and powerful as this. I know Bill Waddell, and I knew his lovely wife, Linda. Yet I knew only about 10 percent of what's in this marvelous book. Once I started, I couldn't stop. It made me laugh, cry, and marvel all at the same time. I loved every syllable of it."

—Gilbert "Bud" Schill, author of *Not Exactly Rocket Scientists and Other Stories* and its sequel, as well as numerous short stories

"Love is both the most durable and mercurial part of the deepest relationships. William Waddell and his wife have a true love story that will make you smile and remember what true love is, warts and all. His story made me feel grateful for my own love story and, importantly, to not take it for granted. His words are one of the best tributes to a spouse I have ever read. It left me resonant with appreciation and gratitude for love."

—Marie Newman, author of *A Life Made from Scratch*

Woven as One
by William R. Waddell

© Copyright 2025 William R. Waddell

ISBN 979-8-88824-812-6

All rights reserved. No part of this publication may be reproduced, stored in a retrieval system, or transmitted in any form or by any means—electronic, mechanical, photocopy, recording, or any other—except for brief quotations in printed reviews, without the prior written permission of the author.

Always On My Mind
Words and Music by Wayne Thompson, Mark James, and Johnny Christopher
Copyright(c) 1971 Screen Gems-EMI Music Inc.
Copyright Renewed
All Rights Administered by Sony Music Publishing (US) LLC, 424 Church Street, Suite 1200, Nashville, TN 37219
International Copyright Secured
Reprinted by Permission of Hal Leonard LLC

Published by
köehlerbooks™

3705 Shore Drive
Virginia Beach, VA 23455
800-435-4811
www.koehlerbooks.com

WOVEN AS ONE

WILLIAM R. WADDELL

VIRGINIA BEACH
CAPE CHARLES

Table of Contents

Author's Note 1
Prologue 3
PART I: THE EARLY YEARS 7
    1: The Very Beginning 9
    2: Williams 13
    3: Our Wedding 16
    4: Law School at UVA 20
PART II: THEMES 29
    5: Hard Work 31
    6: Tolerance 34
    7: Chemistry 36
PART III: LINDA: A TRUE ORIGINAL 41
    8: Just Plain Fun 43
    9: UK and VCU 45
    10: Things Religious 47
    11: Clothes 49
    12: Belly Dancing 51
    13: Of Dogs 53
    14: Daisy and Her Puppies 56
    15: The Kidnapping of Barney 58
    16: Bodie 69
    17: The Bighorn Sheepskin Co. 71
    18: Road Atlanta 73
    19: John Michael 76
    20: Motorcycles and Other Gifts 79
    21: Two Hips and a Back 83
PART IV: PLACES 91
    22: Travels 93
    23: Trains, Long and Short 98
    24: And . . . Cabooses 102

25: Boats: RMS Queen Mary 2 104
26: Somerset, Kentucky 107
27: Big Sur 109
28: Ocean City 113
29: Jacksonville 115
30: Jamaica 118
31: San Salvador 120

Part V: Weaving: Our Connections 127

32: Elizabeth 129
33: Bill's Health 131
34: Kids 133
35: Homes 135
36: Second Homes 139
37: Walking 142
38: Not Monkey Business 144
39: Tennis 147
40: . . . And Automobiles 149
41: The Jaguar 152
42: Friends 156
43: The Dallas Cowboys 159
44: The Fiftieth 162
45: Judy 167
46: New Year's Eve 169
47: Spice 172
48: Valentines and Anniversaries 174
49: A Birthday Letter 179
50: Christmas 181
51: Not All Roses; Clocks 188

PART VI: THE FINAL ACT 195

52: Parting 197
53: Memorials 204
54: Life Alone 208
55: To Linda 211

Acknowledgments 213

Author's Note

QUIRKY AS IT may be, there are times when lowercase letters just don't seem good enough, so I have occasionally used capitalizations to create a kind of quasi-proper noun, as in *Top Dog* or *Best Trip*. Readers who require Proper Style, please forgive me.

Prologue

THIS IS A memoir, you might say, or a very narrow slice of an autobiography, mostly about me and Linda, a wonderful woman with whom I spent about sixty-five years of my life. It will not be chronological, or any other kind of logical for that matter. It's just a recollection of some aspects of our life together, an homage to the love of my life.

My purposes in writing all this down are threefold: First, it is simply an ode to Linda. Second, it is an affirmation to our friends and family that I loved her very deeply. I want readers to know how wonderful a journey it was and how proud I am to have shared it with Linda in the way we did. Third, perhaps describing my feelings and recounting our relationship will in some way help someone understand and appreciate their relationship.

A word about the title. If there is a lesson to be had from our life together, it's this: Two people who enter into a marriage should *together* appreciate and savor every morsel and detail of the relationship, not just selected things or moments or elements of it, because a lot of the richness of a relationship may lie in the sheer *number* of shared memories. I don't mean they should get bogged down in minutia. Her favorite color, what kind of kisses he likes, or that special dinner you shared in San Francisco are details, and remembering them is important. It says you care. Minutia, on the other hand, like how best to load the dishwasher, distract from what really matters. God knows it's not easy to get this distinction right; details and minutia don't come with neat labels.

Weaving is a metaphor that seems helpful to me in understanding how relationships (or at least the relationship this book is about) are built. Weaving typically involves warp and woof, and they may very well be different, each lending its own beauty and strength and maintaining its own character. Also, weaving is inherently granular, and all kinds of intricacies and details are critical if the finished piece is to be as it should: the makeup and types of materials used, loom tensions, colors, patterns, etc. But it probably doesn't matter whether Susie and Bart run the loom exactly the same way, at the same time of day, or whether there are specks of dust on the throw rug. The finished piece is a thing unto itself, and it has its own life and its own purpose. More importantly, the piece may fray or even tear, but it will keep its strength and oneness, and it will survive. The larger the piece, the more threads or filaments or ropes are woven, the more likely it is to survive.

This is surely not a perfect metaphor, nor a brilliant or novel thought, and this book does not pretend to be profound or instructional. I'm only hoping it's halfway readable and maybe serves as an example of how countless, everyday things can be woven into something extraordinary.

Some may ask why this book is mostly about the good times of Linda and Bill, all-American couple, with practically nothing (chapter 51 notwithstanding) about our hurts or disappointments and practically nothing about our stepping on customs and mores. Let me assure you that we had our share of heartaches, our share of departures from norms. But this book is a celebration, not a history or moral analysis. We muddled through our heartaches and skirted around some mores, but through it all, the tapestry of our love, our chemistry, survived.

The super-short version of our story is that Linda and I met in high school when we were fifteen, maybe sixteen, dated sporadically for a while, tried others on for size, grew ever closer for another while, and finally realized, during my last years in college, that we were impossibly in love. We married, had three wonderful boys, lived decades in Richmond, Virginia, then decades in Norfolk, and, with Linda's death, parted, at least for now, when we were eighty.

This book is in six parts, the titles of which speak for themselves. Within each part, the chapters are more or less random, not in order of time or importance, mostly just as they came to me.

I created a draft of parts of this book (maybe 5 percent, including the chapter I called "To Linda") a month or so before she died. I read those parts to her, we cried, and she said, "Only you could have written that," by which I think she meant that it captured something unique between us. I had a nurse read it to her again after she was bedridden, fading in and out, just in case she could hear, even though she wasn't responding. I wanted to be sure she knew how much she, and our life together, meant to me. "To Linda" was read at her memorial service. Although I later modified some other parts, "To Linda" is exactly as I shared it with her. This is our story.

PART I

The Early Years

1

The Very Beginning

IT STARTED IN 1956 in the back seat of a 1946 Ford, but not the way you're thinking. I was a young man of fifteen. My best friend, Dick Smoot, was sixteen and old enough to drive. He had rebuilt the Ford, in which we toured and explored our little town and surroundings every chance we got. Sometimes we weren't doing or looking for anything in particular, but when we were, it often revolved around... girls. At the time in question, neither of us had a steady (or even an unsteady, as I recall), so many a time we fell to talking about which girls were prettiest, most charming, or most... *ahem*... alluring.

The town I grew up in, Fort Thomas, Kentucky, was one of the countless suburbs comprising the Greater Cincinnati area, and in that area, in that time, small suburban towns were fairly insular; Fort Thomas guys dated Fort Thomas girls, Newport guys dated Newport girls, etc. But not exclusively. Especially when there was a good reason, like you met a real looker from a nearby town at your cousin's birthday party, or you saw a cheerleader from a nearby school at a basketball game, which is what happened with me and this girl named Linda. The attraction was immediate, maybe not an Italian *colpo di fulmine* (as described in *The Godfather*), but something like it. She was blond, beautiful, and magnetic. I started thinking about her, naturally, and asking around, and I found out she was the eldest of three beautiful sisters. They lived in neighboring

Newport, very close to the Fort Thomas/Newport line. They were widely known and admired. I wasn't exactly a social butterfly, so I seemed to be one of the few boys who didn't at least know *of* them. Linda, especially, was so pretty and so charming that she was sought after by many a young man in the area, the stuff of many a young man's fantasy.

This popularity probably peaked my interest, but any such peaking was eclipsed by sheer terror, for here I was, a somewhat shy, more-than-somewhat insecure teenage boy, suffering the usual teen angst, consumed with desire but utterly paralyzed by the dreaded fear of rejection. Every time I thought of actually approaching this Goddess of Teendom, I was filled with an icy unease, enough to last from basketball season to warm weather. With the coming of spring, however, my fancy got the better of me, and I agreed to a plan devised by Dick that we thought would provide at least a hope of fulfillment yet spare me the awful risk of rejection. His '46 Ford was a two-door, so the space between the front and back seats was not very visible. We figured that if I hunkered down in the back footwell and pulled a blanket over me, someone outside the car would be unlikely to know I was there.

So, one fine weekend, we put the plan into action. Dick, who knew Linda a little bit from somewhere, drove over to her house, me in the back, duly hunkered and hidden, and blew the horn. In those days, at least in Kentucky, it was okay to do that, even in the case of polite boys and respectable girls, and sure enough, Linda came down the steps in front of her house (although of course I couldn't see). Dick struck up a chat about Elvis or Eisenhower or something, but then slowly worked it around to our respective schools, mutual friends, etc. When the opportunity arose, he somehow managed to work my name into the conversation, and then, using skills I never realized he had, he managed to elicit from Linda whether she knew of me and (drum roll) what she thought.

In all honesty, I don't remember her exact words, but on a scale of zero (revulsion) to ten (attraction), it was something like a six. Maybe "Oh yeah, I've seen him; he's okay" or "Yeah, my sister says he's nice." Just enough to convince me she might not . . . probably wouldn't . . . laugh and hang up if I called her.

Eventually we drove away, and after we conferred, Dick agreed that I had reason to be cautiously encouraged. Emboldened, I called Linda, she agreed to a date (I have no idea where we went), and thus began one of the greatest love affairs of all time, or at least in my experience. But before I go any further with that, I need to revisit the thing about dating "outsiders," i.e., those not from your town. It's fair to say that Fort Thomas, where I was from, was especially given to this insularity. It had a more affluent demographic, set a lot of store by things like education and "success," and may have been a tiny bit haughty about itself. This didn't go unnoticed by those in the surrounding area. In fact, people from Fort Thomas were known as Cake Eaters, after the famous comment attributed to Marie Antoinette.[1] So my dating Linda didn't go unnoticed at Highlands, the high school in Fort Thomas, and was the subject of some muttering and murmuring, especially among the girls.

Perhaps it wouldn't have been *that* noticeable, except that I invited Linda to the Junior Prom. I was a class officer, and an attendant and all that, which made it more notorious, but even so, it might have soon slipped into Old News if not for the fact that it appeared in the *newspaper*. In those days, newspapers, even in larger cities, published a lot of reports of social events, weddings, etc. The *Kentucky Post*, for whatever reason, chose to feature the Highlands High School Junior Prom of 1957 and chose me and Linda and two friends as the photo subjects for the article. I got a lot of teasing about it, but Linda felt the chill of being regarded as a sort of outsider. She was the soul of friendliness and congeniality and was hurt by being ostracized (today we might say "othered") as a "Newport Girl."

---

1   There is even a book about Fort Thomas based on this epithet: Cake Town, USA, by Craig M. Brown (1991).

It was not until many, many years later that I learned how deeply this and other petty slights went in her mind. I was MC at our sixtieth class reunion in 2018 and told the tale of how Linda and I had "met" in Dick's car, just as an amusing anecdote. I ended by saying how grateful I was to Dick and his '46 Ford because they were the key to finding the love of my life. My classmates loved the story and told Linda how sweet it was. But later, back at the hotel, Linda cried and told me how she felt, for the first time, really accepted. After all those years. Made me sad that I hadn't known but glad I had told the story publicly.

Anyway, with a false start or two, a bit of sampling, just to see what other fish were in the sea, and a sort of college break, we remained together for sixty-five years. Over that time, my love for Linda, as cheerleader, wife, mom, lover, tennis partner, helper, and everything else she has been to me, only grew and deepened and became more certain. We shared enough people, things, foreign lands, and sunsets to last a hundred couples. All thanks to that 1946 Ford.

2

Williams

MY UNDERGRADUATE COLLEGE was Williams College, in Williamstown, Massachusetts, which is a long way from Fort Thomas, and in any case it was the time during which we were dating others, so Linda and I didn't really share too much of my Williams experience. But two exceptions come to mind, one in person and one electronic.

First, the electronic. Back then, at least at Williams, individual dorm or fraternity house rooms didn't have telephones. The only phone, typically, was in a common area, often a pay phone—yes, the kind you put coins in. The other fact salient to this story is that "long distance" was a thing. Any call outside a local area had to be paid for individually, through a billing to the phone from which the call was made, coins inserted into a pay phone, or the now almost-extinct "collect call," where the operator (if you don't know who this is, ask your parents) rang the destination phone and asked whether the recipient was willing to accept the charges for the call. This was also referred to as "reversing the charges."

So here we were, hundreds of miles apart, falling (in the last year or two) seriously in love, unable to talk except at rates we couldn't afford. I can't remember if we devised this scheme or stumbled upon it, but we found a way. The scam worked like this: The phone in my fraternity house was an old-fashioned pay phone. Linda would place a collect call to that phone. The custom in the house was that whoever answered the phone would yell for whomever it was for. When I was hunted down and picked up the phone, the operator would ask if I would accept a collect call from Linda Waddle (her maiden name, believe it or not), and I would, of course, say yes. The operator would then ask if this was a pay phone, and I would, of course, say that it was not. Yes, kids, I lied, and I hope the statute has run on whatever crime I was committing.

In those days, in that place, apparently, they had no way to verify electronically whether a pay phone was involved. In any case, we got away with it for a while. The first few times we did it, we kept it brief, but as time went on and we heard no repercussions, we had many long, sometimes lovelorn, conversations.

But one day it came to a head. The house treasurer discovered that the house pay phone had been charged with hundreds—yes, even in those days, *hundreds*—of dollars in long-distance charges from some number in Kentucky. Everyone knew I was from Kentucky, so I had to fess up. I had no money, as usual. I don't remember whether I paid it off in payments or simply stiffed Phi Gamma Delta. If the latter, I'm sorry, and I hope the statute has run on that too.

The other exception was in person. The biggest social event at Williams in those days was Winter Houseparties, when the boys (Williams was all boys then) invited girls for a weekend of dinners, dances, sleigh rides, sporting events, etc. I need to pause here to explain the absence of sex, alcohol, drugs, and rock 'n' roll from this list. The latter two hadn't really hit yet; the first two take a little explanation.

As to sex, the college needed to prevent its Houseparties Weekends from getting a bad reputation. Remember, these were the days before the sexual revolution. Parents of young women (and even young men) would have been horrified by coed dorms. To induce parents of college-age girls to allow them to scurry off to a weekend with a boy in the mountains of Western Mass, the college was at some pains to maintain propriety. So girls (who were mostly from of zero (revulsion) to ten (attraction), it was something like a six. Maybe "Oh yeah, I've seen him; he's okay" or "Yeah, my sister says he's nice." Just enough to convince me she might not . . . probably wouldn't . . . laugh and hang up if I called her.

Eventually we drove away, and after we conferred, Dick agreed that I had reason to be cautiously encouraged. Emboldened, I called Linda, she agreed to a date (I have no idea where we went), and thus began one of the greatest love affairs of all time, or at least in my experience. But before I go any further with that, I need to revisit the thing about dating "outsiders," i.e., those not from your town. It's fair to say that Fort Thomas, where I was from, was especially given to this insularity. It had a more affluent demographic, set a lot of store by things like education and "success," and may have been a tiny bit haughty about itself. This didn't go unnoticed by those in the surrounding area. In fact, people from Fort Thomas were known as Cake Eaters, after the famous comment attributed to Marie Antoinette.[1] So my dating Linda didn't go unnoticed at Highlands, the high school in Fort Thomas, and was the subject of some muttering and murmuring, especially among the girls.

Perhaps it wouldn't have been *that* noticeable, except that I invited Linda to the Junior Prom. I was a class officer, and an attendant and all that, which made it more notorious, but even so, it might have soon slipped into Old News if not for the fact that it appeared in the *newspaper*. In those days, newspapers, even in larger cities, published a lot of reports of social events, weddings, etc. The *Kentucky Post*, for whatever reason, chose to feature the Highlands High School Junior Prom of 1957 and chose me and Linda and two friends as the photo subjects for the article. I got a lot of teasing about it, but Linda felt the chill of being regarded as a sort of outsider. She was the soul of friendliness and congeniality and was hurt by being ostracized (today we might say "othered") as a "Newport Girl."

---

1   There is even a book about Fort Thomas based on this epithet: Cake Town, USA, by Craig M. Brown (1991).

It was not until many, many years later that I learned how deeply this and other petty slights went in her mind. I was MC at our sixtieth class reunion in 2018 and told the tale of how Linda and I had "met" in Dick's car, just as an amusing anecdote. I ended by saying how grateful I was to Dick and his '46 Ford because they were the key to finding the love of my life. My classmates loved the story and told Linda how sweet it was. But later, back at the hotel, Linda cried and told me how she felt, for the first time, really accepted. After all those years. Made me sad that I hadn't known but glad I had told the story publicly.

Anyway, with a false start or two, a bit of sampling, just to see what other fish were in the sea, and a sort of college break, we remained together for sixty-five years. Over that time, my love for Linda, as cheerleader, wife, mom, lover, tennis partner, helper, and everything else she has been to me, only grew and deepened and became more certain. We shared enough people, things, foreign lands, and sunsets to last a hundred couples. All thanks to that 1946 Ford.

2

Williams

MY UNDERGRADUATE COLLEGE was Williams College, in Williamstown, Massachusetts, which is a long way from Fort Thomas, and in any case it was the time during which we were dating others, so Linda and I didn't really share too much of my Williams experience. But two exceptions come to mind, one in person and one electronic.

First, the electronic. Back then, at least at Williams, individual dorm or fraternity house rooms didn't have telephones. The only phone, typically, was in a common area, often a pay phone—yes, the kind you put coins in. The other fact salient to this story is that "long distance" was a thing. Any call outside a local area had to be paid for individually, through a billing to the phone from which the call was made, coins inserted into a pay phone, or the now almost-extinct "collect call," where the operator (if you don't know who this is, ask your parents) rang the destination phone and asked whether the recipient was willing to accept the charges for the call. This was also referred to as "reversing the charges."

So here we were, hundreds of miles apart, falling (in the last year or two) seriously in love, unable to talk except at rates we couldn't afford. I can't remember if we devised this scheme or stumbled upon it, but we found a way. The scam worked like this: The phone in my fraternity house was an old-fashioned pay phone. Linda would place a collect call to that phone. The custom in the house was that whoever answered the phone would yell for whomever it was for. When I was hunted down and picked up the phone, the operator would ask if I would accept a collect call from Linda Waddle (her maiden name, believe it or not), and I would, of course, say yes. The operator would then ask if this was a pay phone, and I would, of course, say that it was not. Yes, kids, I lied, and I hope the statute has run on whatever crime I was committing.

In those days, in that place, apparently, they had no way to verify electronically whether a pay phone was involved. In any case, we got away with it for a while. The first few times we did it, we kept it brief, but as time went on and we heard no repercussions, we had many long, sometimes lovelorn, conversations.

But one day it came to a head. The house treasurer discovered that the house pay phone had been charged with hundreds—yes, even in those days, *hundreds*—of dollars in long-distance charges from some number in Kentucky. Everyone knew I was from Kentucky, so I had to fess up. I had no money, as usual. I don't remember whether I paid it off in payments or simply stiffed Phi Gamma Delta. If the latter, I'm sorry, and I hope the statute has run on that too.

The other exception was in person. The biggest social event at Williams in those days was Winter Houseparties, when the boys (Williams was all boys then) invited girls for a weekend of dinners, dances, sleigh rides, sporting events, etc. I need to pause here to explain the absence of sex, alcohol, drugs, and rock 'n' roll from this list. The latter two hadn't really hit yet; the first two take a little explanation.

As to sex, the college needed to prevent its Houseparties Weekends from getting a bad reputation. Remember, these were the days before the sexual revolution. Parents of young women (and even young men) would have been horrified by coed dorms. To induce parents of college-age girls to allow them to scurry off to a weekend with a boy in the mountains of Western Mass, the college was at some pains to maintain propriety. So girls (who were mostly from out of town) stayed in the homes of Williamstown residents. I don't remember whether staying in a motel was actually forbidden, but I can't remember anyone doing so. And it was strictly forbidden to have a girl in a fraternity house except during prescribed hours. Therefore, sex-wise, everything was, at least on the surface, very proper.

Alcohol was something else. The backdrop is that it's February. It's cold. Students have suffered through a long New England winter. There is snow on the ground. Dorm units and fraternities are making huge creations from ice and snow in hopes of winning the Best Ice Sculpture prize. Last-minute dates have been arranged. The atmosphere is a little electric, anticipating a sort of breakout. Just next door, in New York, it is legal to drink (and buy booze and bring it back to Williamstown) at eighteen. If ever there was a setting that begged for alcohol, this was it. And as far as anyone was able to figure out, the (distinctly) unstated policy of Williams College toward the demon rum was to wink at it. Within limits. So parties were often pretty free-flowing.

Linda and I probably imbibed, but our memories of Houseparties Weekend are not about that, although perhaps a drink or two helped create our fond recollections. It was the first time she had been to Williams, we were rapidly getting serious, and the whole thing can only be described as magic. Linda's spectacular blond good looks and Midwestern charm (she was, after all, runner-up in the Miss Kentucky pageant) took my fraternity brothers by storm. We danced to one of the huge big bands of the day, Richard Maltby, walked around the very New England Williams campus, found places to make out, and, I think, fell irrevocably in love.

3

Our Wedding

BY THE TIME I graduated from Williams in June, we were engaged and had set a date. It is traditional for church weddings to be held in the bride's church, but Linda and I were married in the little white church *I* was attending at the time, in Fort Thomas. I don't remember exactly why, but perhaps it was because we had gone there together a few times, or maybe because we had more friends and family in Fort Thomas. Or perhaps because my church was well set up for a reception on the premises, and hers was not. In any case, on August 25, 1962, a warm Saturday, we were married very traditionally: women in pretty dresses, men in white dinner jackets, with my high school choral director singing "One Hand, One Heart" from *West Side Story*, which can still break me up. The ceremony itself is imprinted in my memory, although other details are a blur.

The church itself was not very big, but it was pretty full. I remember looking out and marveling that so many people wanted to see me get married. There was one invitation, however, that was conspicuously declined. John F. Kennedy had recently been elected president, in the first election in which Linda and I had been eligible to vote. JFK and Jackie were the epitome of beauty and elegance, and I decided they should be invited to our wedding. Linda was somewhat scandalized by this idea, fearing (correctly) that if anyone found out, we would look like presumptuous fools. My argument was that it was a harmless lark, and the White House social secretaries wouldn't know whether we knew the Kennedys or not. As it turned out, I was right. We received a proper "regret," addressed in beautiful handwriting to Linda's address, stating that President and Mrs. Kennedy would be unable to attend. I still have it.

The reception was in the basement of the church. Having a wedding reception there was much more common then than it is now, particularly in small towns, but there was an additional reason Linda made that choice. My parents were teetotalers, with a capital T, and having a reception in a ballroom or country club (neither of our parents belonged to one anyway) would have made the absence of alcohol awkward at best. Also, neither we nor our families would have been financially able to put on such an event. So it was a fairly spartan affair, but there were decorations and a cake, and everything went fine.

Some of my groomsmen were my fraternity brothers from Williams, though, so they were no doubt accustomed to more Big City ways, Westchester County or Philadelphia Main Line. They never said, and I never asked, what they thought of the wedding, but I wouldn't be surprised if they hit a bar or two that night.

I must now admit to something few people, even our closest family and friends, know. Linda and I were married twice. Legally. While I don't honestly remember all the details and nuance, I remember that it was my idea. Here's the story: In the first part of August, Linda and I had a fight—a significant one (I have no idea what it was about). Everyone knows what makeup sex is. This was a makeup marriage. We were both stressed out, I guess, over the prospect of breaking up, given the fact that invitations had gone out, etc., so tears were being shed, and emotions were running pretty high. As sometimes happens, an intense lovers' quarrel leads to an intense reconciliation. I think it scared both of us that we had come close to separating, and when I suggested sealing our marriage immediately, without delay, that scare was just fresh enough to make her receptive to what was by any measure a harebrained idea. We already had a license, so one Saturday, we found a justice of the peace (Edgar Lemker was his name) and, with his wife as witness, tied the knot. They probably judged from the circumstances and rush that Linda was pregnant, but they were very gracious. Linda and I remembered that little ceremony vividly for the rest of our lives, but it was a well-kept secret.

Our honeymoon was in keeping with our financial position, i.e., rather modest. We had planned (hoped) to go to La Citadelle, a famous resort near Hazard, Kentucky, but it was far out of reach cost-wise, so we settled for a tour of Eastern Kentucky that included Natural Bridge State Park and Breaks Interstate Park, on the Virginia line. Doesn't sound like much now, but at the time, it was everything a honeymoon should be, as close to magical as you can get.

Now I will skip ahead a year because I need to recount a tragedy that was related to our wedding, even though it happened later. It's sort of a custom, then and now, to save a piece of your wedding cake and eat it on your first anniversary, so we wrapped up a piece and took it with us to Charlottesville, where we were going to live. When we started settling into our little apartment, however, we discovered that the refrigerator had only a tiny little freezer compartment, barely big enough to hold a couple of ice trays and nowhere near large enough for a large piece of cake. The best alternative we could find (or at least the one we found) was a massive commercial freezer facility, probably used by meat packers or something. There was no retail space or counter, but we found someone who seemed to be in charge and asked if we could store our piece of wedding cake. We may have even begged a little, telling the story of being from out of town, poor students, etc. We were delighted when they said they would keep it and even said it would be free of charge. They probably charged by the ton and didn't quite know how to price our little cake.

Of course, when we went back a year later, they couldn't find the cake. We had been looking forward to our one-year anniversary feast and were very disappointed. They probably had a hanging beef section and a bulk ice-cream section, but no wedding cake piece section, and it had been lost in the shuffle. Oh well.

Before leaving the wedding topic, I have to disclose that Linda and I were actually married *three* times. In August 1987, Linda said we should have a twenty-fifth anniversary party. She took charge of the details, such as time, place, guest list, etc., but we worked together on it to some extent, so it wasn't really a surprise. What *was* a surprise was that she had invited a guy named Dennis Hawley. Dennis was a dear friend, a psychologist by trade, who also happened to be an ordained minister, although during the time we knew him, he was into counseling, not so much saving. Linda and I had consulted with him together during some tough times, and he really had become a great friend and coach. There was an arch with flowers and a regular wedding ceremony, about which the guests (but not I) had been told in advance, Dennis performed the ceremony, and I made a little speech, telling the guests how much I loved Linda for doing all this *and* for putting up with me for twenty-five years.

4

Law School at UVA

AFTER WE GOT BACK from our honeymoon, we set out virtually immediately for Charlottesville, Virginia, and the Law School at the University of Virginia. My family and Linda had attended my Williams graduation, and on our way back, we stopped for a little scouting in Charlottesville. We visited the Student Aid office to figure out how to pay my tuition, found an apartment, and generally got the lay of the land, so when we arrived in September, we were more or less ready to start school.

Law school is a strange and wonderful experience, and in some ways it is unlike any other form of higher education. There is a ton of memorization, although perhaps not as much as med school, with helpings of political science, commerce, history, writing, public speaking, and, most importantly, analysis and puzzle-solving. It is this unusual combination that makes it unique and challenging. This is not the place to dwell on my law school years, but I need to salute the role Linda played; without her, it would have been a different experience altogether.

First, she was my partner and helper in the necessities of life. Getting me to class and back (our apartment wasn't within walking distance of the law school), handling domestic duties, keeping track of finances, and other everyday tasks fell to her.

But beyond that, she was a kind of academic muse. She took a genuine interest in the sometimes strange concepts I had to deal with and the mechanics of this new style of learning. For example, "case studies." Most law school classes, at least in the first year or two, are taught by analyzing court cases. The study of "precedent" cases, why they're important and when and how they apply to current controversies, is a very important part of understanding the law, but it doesn't come naturally. I remember getting my first set of "casebooks" before going to any classes and being mystified by the process. In those first days and weeks, Linda was extraordinarily helpful. She would ask common-sense questions about what a given case was trying to say and why it mattered and make me explain in plain English what the funny abbreviations and numbers in the "citation" of a case (identifying what court decided it, when, etc.) really meant. At the time, it was just part of drinking from the fire hose, but I realize better now that having to explain these things to her sometimes exposed the fact that I didn't really know what I thought I knew, and it *always* helped me be more articulate and logical.

All in all, those were great years for us. As I said, we lived in a tiny basement apartment, but it opened out onto a sort of terrace, so we did have at least some natural light. We shared cooking (although meals were pretty simple and spartan) and cleaning and other duties. We couldn't afford a TV, so we spent a lot of Each Other time, reading, studying, and exploring the Charlottesville area. We had law school friends and went to movies, etc., but they were generally as poor as we were, so our socializing was simple too.

Once, maybe during the summer, we decided to go to Virginia Beach to see the ocean. Linda had seen it on a spring vacation in Florida, but I never had, so off we went. We got there way after dark. Not being able to afford a hotel room, we found a parking place overlooking the beach and snoozed in the car until the sun came up. We held hands and kissed, and I'll never forget the beauty of that sunrise over the ocean with Linda.

Linda was also instrumental in one of my most important life decisions: where to go to work after law school. I considered jobs in New York, Atlanta, and Washington, but she encouraged me to stay in Virginia, with the firm we both worked for (more about this later). The prospect of working for a big national firm or corporation was powerful, but our firm was a very good one, we knew the people, they wanted us, and we liked Virginia. In the end, I listened to her, and it was one of the best decisions I ever made. It offered quality of practice, quality of life, and reasonable financial reward, and I avoided some of the selfishness and ruthless competition that the other choices might have involved. Linda may not have expressed her views just this way, but her instincts were spot-on.

Linda: First Grade

Linda at Fourteen

Miss Kentucky Pageant 1961

Linda and Bill: Married on August 25, 1962

Our Twenty-Fifth Anniversary Celebration

PART II

Themes

THERE WERE THEMES that permeated our years together. They were the "meta" of our connection, the threads that ran through who we were to each other. They weren't perfectly consistent, we didn't always get them right, and we wouldn't have been able to describe them if you had asked. But they were, in some sense, at least as I look back, our North Stars.

5

Hard Work

WORK IS ONE of the things that made our life together richer. Linda and I worked hard, sometimes in similar ways, but more often in different ways. We are absolute polar opposites on the Myers-Briggs test. I am an INTJ—driven, analytical, introverted, and judgmental—while Linda was creative, sensory, extroverted, and entirely nonjudgmental (except of me, of course, but that doesn't count). But true to her basic nature as giver and friend, she included *my* need to accomplish and *my* need to excel among *her* lodestars as well.

A great example was when I was in law school at the University of Virginia. We were dirt poor. Our friends and family wondered aloud how we were going to eat, let alone pay tuition or have a place to live. I had saved a little money from my summer job, and we planned to take with us an industrial-sized bag of rice, of all things, so we told people that if worse came to worst, we would survive on rice and beans. That bag, some clothes, and a little furniture our parents had given us were literally all we had. We somehow secured a little basement apartment, and almost as soon as we had unloaded, Linda was out looking for a job. Her smarts, experience, and looks soon landed her one, at a local manufacturer. My part-time job bussing tables (and later a construction job in the summer) added a little, and we borrowed all we could in the way of student loans, but Linda's hard work was what allowed us to survive. She was the principal homemaker and financial nickel-squeezer, and after classes started, she typed case briefs for me every night to help me prepare. Looking back on it, we had every right to sink, but we didn't.

Perhaps the biggest factor in our finances (short- and long-term) was when Linda landed a job at the Battle law firm. John Battle was a former Virginia governor, and his law firm in Charlottesville was considered one of the best. By the time we got to Charlottesville in 1962, his firm had merged with a Richmond firm and become even more prestigious. Linda had never been a "legal secretary," but she charmed her way into an interview and test, and of course she got the job, which paid better than the one she had. A few months later, she learned that the firm was looking for a part-time student law clerk. She suggested to the managing partner that I would be a good candidate. By then, everyone was halfway in love with her, so I got an interview and was hired.

The Battle firm, with a couple of name changes, was the firm with which I made my fifty-year career. Linda and I often told people we could never get divorced because she would claim every dollar of my success was her doing. And she would have been right.

Later, after law school, she worked as hard as I did. For the first few years, even after our first son was born, it was outside the home. She would have had trouble working for a private law firm because of possible conflicts, so she took a job as assistant to an executive officer at a Fortune 500 company headquartered in Richmond. After our second son's birth, she stayed home and worked toward her own goals, like homemaking and kids and stuff that fifties' women were *supposed* to work at, but also at helping, putting up with, and finding ways to be a partner in all the stuff *I* thought was important, like achievement and production and reward. There were a lot of examples, but one I remember very vividly was in 1980 or so. I was in the very midst of growing and driving my practice, which meant spending a lot of time "on the road" in Boston or New York or LA or wherever, spending very long hours wherever I was, and being under a lot of stress. I had just finished a particularly punishing period, closed the deal, and headed home.

Linda was good at detecting stress levels, and the next day she announced that I was going to unwind. She had planned, down to the last detail, several days in Bermuda, somewhere I had never been. I was packed, ticketed, driven to the airport, and taken care of for those few days. It took me the first couple to come down, but the trip was a great success, not only as decompression and disconnection but just enjoyment. I came back rejuvenated and ready for the next hill in a way I would have never done on my own.

I tried to help Linda in the things she worked on, but truth be told, she gave far more as a helper than I did. At the time, I vastly undervalued Linda's importance in my achievements. All that support in school, all those early mornings and late nights and business dinners and trips, with her holding down the fort. Thanks, honey, and I'm sorry I didn't say it enough at the time. The net result and silver lining, though, was that all this working and helping and putting-up-with ultimately brought us closer, made us appreciate the importance of what the other was doing. Work can be a stressor and a drag, but it can also be a source of sharing and mutuality. We were lucky enough to mostly experience the latter.

6

Tolerance

TOLERANCE IS ONE of those concepts that is easily oversimplified and easily abused. Too little of it, obviously, is deadly to any relationship, be it personal, societal, political, or otherwise, leading to friction, war, divorce, etc., and too much of it can mean an unfair advantage and/or "enabling." Linda and I, like all couples, had things that had to be negotiated. Also like all couples, sometimes we failed to do so successfully, and we had to find an off-ramp or a way to forget or forgive or just suck it up and get over it. But sometimes we were successful, and if there was a keystone of these times, it was tolerance.

Linda gets much more credit for this than I do. The things that called for tolerance on my part were, by and large, not things that were complex or hard to understand or laden with emotion. Linda's proclivity for buying clothes? Not insignificant, and perhaps resistant to solution, but you could *see* a solution even if it was hard to implement.

The things Linda had to tolerate, though, were harder. They grew out of my personality and ambition, my very makeup. Hard things to change. Like my proclivity to kill snakes (about which I'll talk more in chapter 11), an intensity about things, and a tendency to take on everything.

My career was bad enough. I thought any assignment had to be done today, and it had to be perfect. Often, I would stay at my office late into the evening. Sometimes I would come home after business hours, have dinner, and maybe take one of the kids on a bike ride, but then I would return to the office. Saturday morning work was expected, but most often Saturday afternoon and/or Sunday were office days as well. This was especially true in the early years, as it is with many lawyers in big firms, but even after I had been in practice for decades, I still put in a lot of office time *and* a lot of travel. I became heavily involved in firm management and had two offices, one in Northern Virginia and one in Richmond, for a couple of years. Hours on top of hours.

All that would have perhaps been manageable but for all the other stuff I got involved in. At every turn, I fell into the chairmanship of this or the presidency of that. Everything from professional associations to schools to community associations to charities. And having a top leadership post meant that I couldn't just attend *most* meetings; I had to be at *all* of them, sitting in on committee or task force meetings as well. To top it off, I taught classes at a community college and later at UVA Law School, and I served on the boards of several businesses. Again, these were command performances, so I had to schedule around them.

The only reason I list these things is to indicate the incredible tolerance Linda had for my attention to them. In writing this book, I looked back at my old desk calendars and was astonished by the sheer congestion on them—day after day and night after night. I marvel at Linda's ability not only to tolerate it but to support and enhance it. As with hard work, tolerating each other three bearishly (not too little, not too much) isn't a strain; it brings you closer, or at least it did us.

7

Chemistry

THE THIRD THEME is chemistry. One time a good friend of mine who was going through hard times in his marriage asked me what the secret was to staying together. I immediately said *chemistry*, by which I was trying to describe the indefinable, gut-level, overriding connection that two people have. Not just a physical connection, although that certainly can be part of it. Rather, a glue that survives disagreements, temporary anger, disappointment, or even betrayal.

Poets can describe this feeling, but I'm no poet. The closest I was able to come to capturing it in a few words was in the inscription on a clock, an inscription that became a sort of touchstone for us. You'll find it later in this book, if you get that far. But whatever it is, Linda and I had it. It was in our fabric. I'll try to recount a couple of the ways in which it revealed itself.

I don't know exactly how it started, but sunset was a thing for us. For as far back as I can remember, we always enjoyed watching it together, sometimes holding hands, sometimes talking about the colors, and sometimes just watching and thinking about things we didn't make time for otherwise: things like lyrics, spirits, beauty, nature, and each other. Mostly each other. When the sun was gone, I don't think we felt loss, just the end of something peaceful; we knew there would be another one.

Sometimes sunsets were effortless, like in Big Sur or on board a ship. But other times we had to work at it. Because of the way our houses in Richmond and Norfolk were situated, we didn't really have a sunset at either of them, and life is busy with mundane matters like finishing yard work at that time of day. Sometimes we hunted up an open view or went up to my office, which is in a tall building, but not often. When we were traveling, though, free of cooking and yarding, we relished that time of day and looked forward to experiencing it. If others were with us, we were pretty insistent (probably annoying) that sunset come first in terms of planning. Distance, dinnertime, interference with activities etc., just had to yield. I remember one time we had a really important business cocktail party on a terrace on the east side of the hotel around sunset time. I was chair or past president or some damn thing, but we just snuck out. Simple as that. Maybe we were missed, maybe we missed a good client, maybe not. But we decided sunset had priority that night. We found a spot on the west side of the hotel, even a bench (sort of), and enjoyed our purloined glass of wine. It was better than business. Sometimes we had to work really hard, like the time we had to get in our rental car, buy some mini splits of wine at a convenience store, and drive all over town searching for a decent view, but by golly, we found a spot before the sun was completely gone. Good for us.

Our beach house[2] has a deck off the third floor, which faces west, what we came to call the Sunset Deck. We "did sunset" there innumerable times, usually with a glass of wine, sometimes with guests and sometimes alone, but always with a feeling, conscious or not, that this was a special place for us. It's not like the view is anything special, certainly not like a tropical dip into the sea through palm trees, but it sees a sunset that was good enough for us—sort of an open view over trees and houses—and it made us feel like we were sharing something intimate and special . . . because it was ours.

The closeness we felt because of our sunset custom was priceless. We saw sunsets all over the world, I guess, from the top of the old World Trade Center to above the Arctic Circle in July, where sunset

---

2 See Part V.

was almost there but never came. Wherever I am, I will always think of Linda at sunset and recall the way we shared it.

The other thing that may help describe what I mean by chemistry is songs. I guess most couples have a song or maybe more than one. Lots of them come during the starry-eyed courtship days, but ours was later, maybe in our forties, when we began to realize how much we really meant to each other, and how deeply we were connected, but how many opportunities we had missed to say so. Along came Willie Nelson with his classic "Always on My Mind," and it became Our Song. The lyrics so beautifully and perfectly express our realized love that I have to recite them here:

> Maybe I didn't love you
> Quite as often as I could have
> And maybe I didn't treat you
> Quite as good as I should have
> If I made you feel second-best
> Girl I'm sorry I was blind
> You were always on my mind
> You were always on my mind
> And maybe I didn't hold you
> All those lonely, lonely times
> And I guess I never told you
> I'm so happy that you're mine
> Little things I should have said and done
> I just never took the time
> And you were always on my mind
> You were always on my mind

We heard that song live at a Willie concert in Fresno, California, a few years ago and held each other and cried like babies, which probably amused those around us. But it says a lot about how connection overcomes inattention and how your heart can be in the right place even if your head isn't. There were points at which Linda and I could have lost each other, but chemistry was there, and we didn't. Not everyone gets that chance.

Finally, yes, chemistry does include physical connection. You won't read much more about that here, it being an intensely and permanently private thing, except to say that Linda and I enjoyed that vital connection throughout our years together. It was fun, complete, fulfilling—some might even say adventuresome—and was the perfect accompaniment to the melodies of everyday life.

PART III

Linda: A True Original

NOW I WANT to tell you a little more about Linda. This part, about her, and part V, about what I have called our "connections," obviously overlap a lot. I was involved in some ways in the things that made her special, and she was part of our connections, but I put these recollections in their own space because they say more about her than about us.

Linda was born in Somerset, Kentucky, but by the time she started school, she and her parents had moved to another Kentucky town, Newport, a midsize suburb of Cincinnati. She always described her upbringing as working or middle class. Their first home in Newport was a row house fronting about twenty feet from the main line of the Norfolk and Western Railway; later they moved to more typical suburban locations.

Her high school years were shaped by her remarkable beauty and charm. After a couple of college years, those qualities led her to modeling and competition in beauty pageants. She was Miss Newport and Miss This and That, which led to the Miss Kentucky pageant, one of the state contests that selected the Miss Universe contestants. Pretty big deal in those days. She was a runner-up, and I always thought she should have won.

I'll leave her "growing up" time that, since our years together were mostly later. The rest of this part is about those years.

8

Just Plain Fun

THAT'S PROBABLY THE FIRST thing most people who knew Linda would say about her: She was just plain fun. Serious when she wanted to be but always easy to be around. Not in a Life of the Party sense or a Look at Me sense. She was just a quintessential extrovert, absorbing energy from where she was and what she was doing and who she was with. Seldom did she not like someone; she wasn't naive or gullible; in fact, she was a shrewd judge of character. But she almost always managed to find something attractive or engaging about other people.

One example I remember was in Puerto Rico, in 1993, at a conference that centered around the Health Security Act being championed by Hillary Clinton. Feelings, pro and con, about this proposal were running very high on the national political scene. The conference we were attending included passionate supporters and equally passionate opponents. At dinner one night, we found ourselves enmeshed in this debate. Some at the table (including Linda) were pro. Others, particularly one guy who represented a large medical insurance group, were opposed, one might even say loudly and bitterly so. Tempers were beginning to flare. The dinner was very elegant, complete with a live Latin band, but the whole political thing threatened to ruin the evening. It was salvaged when Linda asked Loud Guy if he would like to dance. Perhaps taken a little off guard, the guy agreed, and he and Linda, who was a terrific dancer, took the floor. He turned out to be a pretty good dancer himself. Rhumbas, sambas, the works. I got tired just watching and left them on the dance floor. She got back to our room shortly thereafter, raving about what a good time she had. I don't remember whether poisonous politics ever interfered with the social aspects of the meeting again, but I don't think so.

I'll talk more later about the European jaunts she took with some close friends a few years ago. I wasn't along, of course, but I'm told her charm and ability to have fun overcame the most daunting linguistic and cultural barriers. She was an expert at mimicking works of art and was the permanent driver. Wrestling with street signs, negotiating roundabouts, fending off aggressive fellow drivers, and dealing with strange traffic laws were sometimes hair-raising, but they were always sources of fun to her. Once, she won a contest to see who could produce the best sound from one of those eight-foot-long alpenhorns (think Ricola). If there was a camel nearby, she wanted to ride it. She could strike up a conversation with most any stranger without seeming forward or presumptuous, just genuine and friendly.

On a trip that took us to downtown Los Angeles (or maybe Hollywood), we found ourselves near one of those sidewalk grates that blows air, like the one in the famous Marilyn Monroe photos. Linda happened to be wearing a full skirt, the kind Marilyn was wearing, so I told Linda how cute she would look in such a picture. I didn't really expect her to take me up on this crack, but there was no one around, and after a little hesitation, she did it. The result was a series of photos much like the ones of Marilyn, laughing uproariously, skirt blowing up, just plain having fun. Some might say those photos are too racy for publication (and in fact they haven't been until now), but I don't think Linda would mind.

9

UK and VCU

LINDA WAS REALLY SMART. She outwitted me not only with clothes (see later) but in a number of other ways as well. She was always into a renovation, decorating, organizing, or managing, whether it was knitting, stained glass, photography, writing, gardening, reading, cooking, or taking care of cars; she even ran her own retail business at a big shopping mall one Christmas (more later). Some of these were because she enjoyed them, some because she felt they were a part of her job, and some just for the sheer hell of it. I often picked her brain on things that came up in my career, even legal issues, and often she gave me a new angle or insight that was helpful. She was usually good at whatever she attempted.

But structured, formal education wasn't something she put much store by. Although we weren't "going together" at the time, I visited her a couple of afternoons when she was at the University of Kentucky. I found her happy both with her studies and with her life in general. But, as I've noted, after a couple of years, she decided to take a break, go to work, buy a Thunderbird, and enter a beauty pageant or two.

Linda thought of it at the time as a year-or-so hiatus, but as so often happens, it turned into a permanent one. I will always be grateful for the break, whatever it was, because it was during this time that we refound each other, but she always talked about going back to college, completing her degree. Then my plans for law school, our wedding, pure survival, and children came along, and she was unable, practically speaking, to return to school. But later in life, when the kids were mostly out of the house, she decided to reenroll, this time at Virginia Commonwealth University in Richmond, majoring in, of all things, Spanish. Off she went to regular classes and night classes, worrying about things that college students worry about: missing a class, studying for tests, trying to balance other things with her educational pursuit. She was in her forties by then, but so youthful in appearance and so inherently extroverted that she fit in much better than she might have.

Linda really enjoyed those classes, and naturally she did very well academically, made straight A's, and even talked of visiting Spain to gain fluency. But eventually, she lost interest and never finished her degree. Looking back, I think Linda needed challenge, even more than most people do. Although she probably wouldn't have recognized it at the time (I certainly didn't), as soon as she found out she could learn or conquer something, she was ready to move on. I'm glad she didn't move on from me.

10

Things Religious

YOU PROBABLY CAN'T appreciate Linda (or Bill, for that matter) without understanding the part religion played in our lives. Her very early years were in a rural environment, including a rural church. She described the services she went to as a young child, the Pentecostal services, the Sunday atmosphere, getting specially dressed up in clothes she didn't wear anywhere else. She always looked back on that experience as one she enjoyed, but not one that shaped her. In Charlottesville, when I was in law school, everything was at breakneck speed, and we didn't really make time for churchgoing, but when we moved to Richmond, I think we both felt the need for a church affiliation, especially as we looked forward to having children.

We joined a Presbyterian church in Richmond. That was the denomination in which I had been raised and in which we had been married. All of our boys were baptized there, and we attended services regularly. I even taught Sunday School for a while. As time went on, though, the church became more and more fundamentalist. This was during the late '60s and early '70s, when the Jesus Movement, out of California, was gaining a lot of traction, and in some Christian circles, you could be made to feel a little uncomfortable if you weren't noisily "born again." Our church was in that circle, and we felt more and more outside its mainstream. Although we continued to take the boys to church, since we wanted them to have enough Christian background to make up their own minds, our hearts were increasingly not in it.

So, for the rest of our marriage, we could fairly be described as Sunday Christians, sometimes (but not regularly) attending services and sometimes leaning on faith in hard times, but not being "religious." I think she and I looked on religion and spirituality and the mystery of life in somewhat the same way: There are a lot of things we don't know, and we didn't have the certainty (some would say arrogance) to think we did. We were open to learning and listened to spiritual ideas, but we never felt the need to embrace one set of ideas to the exclusion of all others.

I asked Linda about this when she was desperately ill, whether spiritual counseling was something she wanted. She said that it wasn't. I can't remember her exact words, but the gist was that she looked at me and her family and friends as her support. The hospice caregivers asked both of us the same question, and we gave them the same answer.

At Linda's memorial service, my brother Phil, who is a dedicated believer, read Psalm 23, partly because I wanted to include *some* religious content out of respect for believers, but partly because I thought Linda would want to affirm that she found value in spirituality and that her mind was open.

11

Clothes

ONE OF LINDA'S most striking characteristics is how well she wore clothes. Stunning in a formal setting, she was equally arresting in casual wear, a tennis dress, or a swimsuit. She would have probably said she looked better in certain colors, but I thought she looked great in all of them: Linda in a little black dress, Linda in a kelly-green pantsuit, or Linda in blue jeans. She was truly beautiful, always getting second looks regardless of the surroundings.

But.

One of the side effects of (or perhaps a natural accompaniment to) this ability to choose and do justice to apparel was that beginning early and lasting most of her life, Linda bought a bunch of clothes and accessories. A bunch. She was famous for it among her friends, whom she often took along on shopping trips. It became the source of some friction in the Waddell house. The friction was partly mitigated by the fact that I was making a pretty good living, but mostly by Linda's genius at techniques like obscuring new acquisitions ("Oh no, this isn't new; you just never noticed it") or asserting that an item had been or soon would be returned. Another technique, after we had daughters-in-law, was to say an item was destined for *them*, not Linda.

When all else failed, she would hide stuff in a closet I never looked in. A decade or so before she died, her devotion to clothes cooled, and she began giving away her racks of clothes, pocketbooks, shoes, etc., to friends, family, and charity. Because she was going through back and hip surgeries, I helped her with the retrieval, sorting, and boxing. We were startled by the number of things she had buried and forgotten. Many were unworn and still bore a price tag.

Oddly, I actually enjoyed retrieving all these things and was a little sad that Linda hadn't gotten to enjoy them more. After she died, there were plenty left, including her favorites that she had worn many times. Some of my most wrenching moments were going through and giving those clothes away.

12

Belly Dancing

THIS SEEMS LIKE a logical place to mention what was probably Linda's most unlikely accomplishment. I can't remember the time frame, exactly, but perhaps in the '70s or so, belly dancing became sort of a thing. Not a *big thing*, not for *everybody*, but it was appealing enough to the adventurous of heart to make it noticeable. Maybe a little like pole dancing in the early aughts.

And so Linda, always looking for something new, probably intrigued by it being a little racy, got into belly dancing. She joined a studio run by a *real* belly dancer from Egypt and began accumulating the appropriate dresses, jewelry, makeup, and accessories. As I recall, a couple of her friends also got into it, although never as seriously as she did.

Linda had a background in dance. She learned tap and soft-shoe while growing up, and she was a great jitterbugger, even after it became known as shag or swing. Her "talent" in the Miss Kentucky and other beauty pageants was dancing. She was beautiful, athletic, and sensual, all made to order for the belly dancing art form, and I think she was truly good at it, although I only got to see her perform a couple of times.

Her most famous appearance was on the local PBS television station, which presented a recital from the studio where she studied. I remember watching her come out on stage all duded up and diaphanous in a sort of elaborate tank top, something called a hip scarf, bangles, chains, tassels, and, sure enough, a jewel in her belly button. All accompanied by exotic Arabic dance music. You might think the heavy makeup and sparkly attire might have cheapened her natural beauty, but it didn't. I remember thinking how proud I was, not only of her appearance and performance but of her courage and hutzpah to do it. This wasn't something every lady of the Philadelphia Main Line or Richmond West End would do.

1 3

Of Dogs

WE HAD SEVEN DOGS during the time we were together. We loved all of them, but some were more memorable than others. Linda's story wouldn't be complete without them. I love dogs and think I have a bond with the ones we've lived with, but my connection pales in comparison to Linda's. It's another example of her generosity of spirit, her selflessness. She simply craved happiness for her companions. Period. Spoiled them as a result, maybe, but she couldn't have cared less. Experts will tell you all kinds of things about pack pecking orders, alpha and beta dogs, how dogs view humans, etc. Exactly what experts would say about Linda's way with doggies, I'm not sure, but they seemed to sense immediately that Linda was something special. When it came time for a tangible memorial to Linda, I made sure dogs were a part of it because that's what she would have wanted.

This vibe became more intense over the years. It was subtle for a while, but it burst out when our big golden, Barney, tore his ACL and had to be confined for several weeks. Linda cared for that dog like he was her baby. She sat beside his playpen day in and day out and helped him outside for rest stops. She fed him, petted him, talked to him, and just about didn't leave his side. Barney, who for most of his life had been a fairly independent soul (ran loose for the first eight years of his life) yielded to Linda's charms. From then on, he was her dog.

Before Barney, there was Daisy. We'll get to her. After Barney, there were two big Bernese mountain dogs, sometimes known as Berners. For those who are not familiar with the breed, they are large (ours were about 125 pounds) but very gentle. They are long-coated, with distinctive markings that some have said make Berners the most beautiful dogs in the world. They have an unequalled ability to win your heart.

The fact that we picked this breed arose out of a trip to Vancouver. We were in Victoria, a nearby city that is always remembered by the colorful, luxuriant flower boxes that line some of its streets. We were strolling along one of these streets when we happened to spot this beautifully marked white, sable, and black animal, and we both said immediately that we had to see it up close. When we ran over, the owner told us about the breed, and we determined right then and there that we wanted a Berner.

Andy, our first Berner, died when he was four years old of a blood cancer that runs through the breed despite every effort to eliminate it.[3] Losing him was extremely hard on Linda; at one point, she swore she would never have another dog because she couldn't face the trauma of having to part with them.

Fortunately, she got over that, and when we were ready for another dog, she chose another Berner, who we named Teddy. Teddy was a wonderful companion for nine years and the subject of the commissioned painting I will mention in the Christmas chapter.

Barney, Andy, and Teddy spent some time with us at our second home in Sandbridge. I've spoken of the Sunset Deck at that house. It was from that deck (at sunset) that we scattered some of the ashes of those three furry companions. We thought it fitting that they symbolically rest there. Two of our boys were there that weekend, as I recall, and we had a little ceremony, with a eulogy I wrote and a lot of tears.

---

3   His final illness was the reason we had to cut short one of our Jamaica visits.

After Linda died in 2021, I decided to create a permanent memorial that incorporated her love of dogs. It's located near the entrance to the Richmond SPCA and consists of a bronze figure of Linda sitting on a bench with her arm around a small dog. On the ground are two larger dogs, representing Berners and goldens. A plaque describes her love of animals. A fountain and benches are nearby, so both humans and dogs can enjoy the little park. The whole space is designated "Linda's Garden."

14

Daisy and Her Puppies

WE HAD TWO DOGS before Daisy, but they weren't with us long, so you might say she was our first permanent dog. She was an Old English sheepdog, the breed that has bangs over their eyes so you wonder how they can see. I think Linda became enamored of the breed because of a movie from our teenage years, *The Shaggy Dog*, but Daisy was named after the dog who belongs to the Bumstead household in the comic strip *Blondie*. She was a quintessential Old English, happy-go-lucky, loyal, wonderful with kids, and very friendly. That last characteristic, her friendliness, together with three other factors, decidedly changed her life and ours: First, in those days, it was not unusual to allow one's dog to run free, although that practice was coming to an end in many cities. Daisy ran free. Second, she was not spayed. Again, that was not as unusual in those days. Third, there was an unfixed Dalmatian, a big muscular fellow, in our neighborhood. Taken together, this is a brew sure to produce puppies, and sure enough, it did.

Whether we were initially dismayed or happy, I frankly don't remember; maybe it was a mix, but when we found out she was expecting, we went into high gear. The boys were probably about twelve, ten, and eight, the perfect age for puppies. We read up on what needed to be done, laid in supplies, built a whelping box in the garage, complete with radiant heat, and waited. Linda (as you might expect) was the first to recognize the signals. We led Daisy to the prepared area and set up our video camera. We had read that sometimes pregnant dogs become aggressive or anxious, but Daisy was very cooperative, seeming grateful that she was being taken care of.

We thought we knew from our reading what was going to happen, but when the time came for the puppies, we were awestruck. Puppies emerge in clear sacs, with some fluids, and the mother immediately tears open the sac. All at one time (or at least it seemed so for Daisy), she cleans up the afterbirth, licks the puppy awake, and gives it a teat. It is a truly remarkable process, and if you have an ounce of love for animals, it will bring a tear to your eye. Linda was completely transfixed and hovered over the box, making sure everything went right. Not only did it go right; it went right eleven more times. Twelve puppies in all, of which all but one survived. The one who didn't was the runt; we named him Piggy, and we did our best to pull him through, but couldn't, about which Linda and the boys were brokenhearted. But I guess it was at least a good life lesson for the boys.

A whole book could be written about the joys and challenges of raising those pups. Daisy was a wonderful mother, keeping everybody fed and the box and herself remarkably clean. Once in a while we would intervene to bring a little more equity to the feeding situation, but by and large, they worked it out. Nature has a way of doing that. They were all cute (as puppies usually are), and we either sold or found homes for them pretty easily. Actually letting them go was not so easy, but obviously we had to.

This was repeated four more times. Each time, Daisy had ten or twelve puppies. So, over her life, we figure she had between fifty and sixty. I guess we had her spayed eventually, although truthfully, I don't know for sure. Some of her descendants are probably still around. Daisy lived a good, long life, running free until the day she died.

15

The Kidnapping of Barney

WE NOW RETURN to Barney. As with Daisy's puppies, a whole book could be written about Barney; perhaps someday I will. But one event in his life stands out so starkly that it has to be told regardless.

There seem to be (though experts might disagree) two distinct varieties of golden retrievers. One is the show variety: very pretty, light in color, kind of cuddly. Show goldens are wonderful; I have one now (Bodie), and he is truly my best friend. The other variety is more a field or hunting animal: bigger, darker colored, more independent, and somehow more masculine. Barney was prototypically the second variety, and, as with Daisy, we allowed him to keep his original equipment.

Barney ran free, and a part of his free-roaming life was that he went places we didn't know he went. For example, he was extremely accomplished at detecting a female that was "in season," if she was within about a thousand miles of his nose. The first couple of times he didn't come home at night caused us terrible angst, but later we came to understand that these absences probably just meant he was camped out near an intended ladylove's house and simply needed to be brought home and kept in for a few days. A couple of times, we found him in a place that had required him to cross busy four-lane highways. Love conquers all.

Another place (we found out later) he went was "down in the

woods" with dog buddies of his. One of his buddies would actually come to our front door and scratch to see if he could come out and play. We were alerted to where they went by neighbors who saw them disappearing into the brush, but who knows where he went from there. When we were in Sandbridge, we kept him closer to home. He had a big fenced backyard to run in, but once in a while he would escape. His favorite destination was a canal a few blocks from the beach house. He loved water, and when he got half a chance, cold weather or hot, he headed for the canal and came home dripping wet.

Barney was with us in Richmond for several years, then in Norfolk for another several. We learned that his favorite place in Richmond was a strip shopping center about a half mile from our house. His go-to store was a supermarket, where the staff was tolerant and actually came to expect him. He learned that if he stepped on the mat, the door would automatically open, and he could get into the place where all those good smells were. He was a handsome and friendly soul, seemed at home, I'm sure, and despite being in gross violation of store rules and health codes, he was halfway accepted. When it *was* time to show him out, the staff used the usual technique, which was to show him a delicious treat and get him to follow them to the door. Thus, Barney was rewarded for his visit and trained perfectly for the next time. We learned all this later; all we knew was that he was out and about most of the day.

Some of you are thinking by now that Linda and Bill were pretty irresponsible dog owners, and by today's standards, we would have to plead guilty. But the standards were different then, and in any case the statute of limitations has expired. We (and Barney, I guess) received our just desserts when he was kidnapped from that very strip center.

A few hundred feet from Barney's supermarket, there was a McDonald's. Foraging around there, particularly by the patio eating area and drive-through, was probably pretty good for a guy like Barney. There was a lot of foot and car traffic. You can see the trouble coming.

Back to his home lifestyle. He slept at home and was often around during the day (particularly at feeding time), but we didn't expect him to be around all the time. Kind of like kids in the old days during the summer: The only real rules were to stay out of trouble, don't get hurt, and be home for dinner. And in Barney's case, as noted, allowances were made for his manly needs. But when he was gone overnight, particularly multiple nights, we became concerned. Over time, we developed a search routine with graduated levels, like DEFCON 3, DEFCON 4, etc. So when he was MIA for a couple of nights in that summer of 1988, we mounted up for a search.

The first element of our standard search was to stand outside our front door, call him, and whistle. Sometimes he was just hanging out nearby and would come trotting up. The next level was to get in the car and ride around the neighborhood, with the same calls and whistles, and poll some of the neighbors. On this occasion, none of this produced Barney, and by the third night, we were getting really worried. Even his longest *voyage de l'amour* was not this long; by now we should have received a call from someone, or Barney's hunger should have overcome his lust. He had been wearing a collar and tags, of course, but who knows what could have happened to them if he had been in a fight or hit by a car or something. So we found ourselves on a level similar to DEFCON 1, the highest state of alarm. This meant calls to animal control, the police, vets, shelters, etc., even searching ditches alongside busy roads we knew he travelled. Nothing.

For the next few days after that, we distributed "lost dog" flyers with Barney's picture on them. We left one at every shop, business, school, or church that would take it and spent hours posting them on any telephone or pole we could find. Still nothing, so we decided to up the ante with a reward. We created a whole new set of posters, in color no less, with his picture, a description, "$500 Reward," and our phone number.

Five hundred dollars in 1989 got some attention. We began

getting leads. At first, each lead was terribly exciting; we thought, surely, we were going to get our beloved Barney back. But it soon became clear that these leads could be, and in fact were, either mistaken or figments of the imagination.

By now Barney had been gone a couple of weeks. Word had gotten around to our friends, and they knew from our demeanor, if they didn't know before, how much we loved him and how much we were feeling the loss. The expression "You look as if you just lost your best friend" probably described us accurately. But as two weeks became three, reality, as they say, began to set in. We certainly weren't ready to give up; we were still posting flyers and following leads, but the undeniable fact was that hope was fading.

It was in this context of dimming optimism that we decided to throw a Hail Mary. We knew the key to finding Barney, if he was still alive, was getting the word out. What we were hoping was that he was okay, maybe being cared for, but had lost his collar and couldn't find his way home. So our last best chance, we thought, was to advertise in the newspaper classifieds. Back then, classifieds got much more attention than they do now. In fact, it's fair to say they were the primary source for buying, selling, giving notices, etc. We had placed a classified ad fairly early in the process, but it was just an ordinary couple of lines about a "lost dog" and probably didn't get much attention. This time, we sprang for more space, used larger letters, and referred to the $500 reward in the largest font of all.

That ad *did* get attention—and new leads. One caller, I remember, from about five miles away, swore up and down that he had seen a big golden walking along his street. Based on our description, he was sure it was Barney. Five miles was close enough to be plausible but far enough away for him to be lost. We devoted a lot of time to searching and whistling in that area, but to no avail. This and other leads went nowhere.

It had now been over a month. Brokenhearted as we may have been, we were finally ready to admit to each other that Barney was gone. There was grief, guilt, and all the other emotions that go with this sort of loss. I was always more relaxed about letting Barney run loose than Linda was, so she could have reasonably blamed me, but she didn't. We *did* tell each other that if we could do it over, we would be more careful.

I wouldn't say we had given up hope at this point, but almost. The ad had run for two weeks and two weekends, and we hadn't had a new lead in a while. But one Saturday night, we received a call from, of all places, Lynchburg, Virginia, which is a good two hours from Richmond. It was a lady, and she asked first about the reward, then about Barney's appearance, the timing of his disappearance, etc. By this time, the call was getting my attention because of its origin and because the caller seemed to be very interested in specific details. Eventually, she said she thought maybe she knew where Barney was, but she wanted to be sure she was going to get the reward. I assured her that if it turned out to be Barney, we would pay her as promised. She said her cousin had the dog and gave me a name and address.

The address was in Skippers, Virginia, about an hour and a half south of Richmond. Linda and I talked about it and initially decided there just wasn't enough to it to drive that far. But then our lingering perseverance (however thin) prevailed, and we decided to go down there the next afternoon. Part of our thinking was that it was a nice day, and we needed a stress break anyway, so we packed some food and set out, thinking that we would at least have a nice drive and find a place for a picnic. Neither of us was holding out any real hope that we were going to find Barney, and we shared that out loud. On the way down, we talked more about where to picnic than anything else.

Skippers is a tiny town almost to the North Carolina line. I wish I still had the address we were given. I can only remember that it wasn't easy to find. No GPS, of course. The area was semirural; I'm not even sure we had a house number. We cruised around for an hour and essentially gave up, thinking the whole thing was probably a scam anyway. I don't think we were particularly disappointed, only because we hadn't let ourselves get our hopes up. It was late in the afternoon, so we found a place for our picnic.

When we finished our picnic, I said I wanted to have one more try at finding the address, so I drove into a gas station (maybe the only one in Skippers) and asked for help. The guy wasn't really sure, but he gave us some information we hadn't had before, so we thought we would try one more time. Linda seemed a little exasperated with me for insisting we go back; she was convinced it was futile, and it was getting dark. In talking about it over the years, Linda confirmed that she was *more* than exasperated, and she would have headed back to Richmond at that point.

In any case, we drove back to the area where the house was supposed to be, and this time (maybe with the gas station guy's info) we found a house that seemed like it might be the one. And there was a chain-link fence enclosing an area adjacent to the front yard. And there was a big dog standing in the enclosed area. And he looked like Barney.

We both just sat there, in the fading afternoon light, and looked. We were caught between our joy and relief at perhaps finding our long-lost Barney and our fear and anxiety that it wasn't him. We were frozen not only by these conflicting emotions but also by the practicalities. We didn't really know this homeowner, and we didn't know if his cousin had alerted him. The fence might or might not have a gate, and it might or might not be locked. The dog could be a vicious guard dog for all we knew.

I finally decided to approach the house. There didn't seem to be much activity, so we weren't sure whether anyone was home. I rang the bell. No answer. I rang again. Still no answer. Linda had stayed in the car, being a little apprehensive about the whole scene. I turned and looked toward her, hoping she would give me some instructions, but of course she didn't. All this time, the dog had been quiet. No pacing, no barking. Looking back on it, this would have been unusual for a rural dog near nightfall, but it was actually quite typical for Barney. He was always very calm, very confident. He would stand up for himself if given trouble, but otherwise was rather stoic.

I walked over to the fence, maybe twenty-five feet away. It was chain-link, well-made, four feet high, and it did have a gate, with a latch but no lock. The closer I got, the surer I became that the dog was Barney, although he was just standing there, looking at me really closely but not seeming to know me. I had a decision to make: Should we take him with us or wait for the person who lived in the house? Just then, the dog, who was just standing stock still, made a whimpering sound, the little whine dogs sometimes give when they want something, and I decided we had come this far and were going to take him home. If we had to bring him back or straighten something out, we would do it later.

I opened the gate, and he came right with me. When I opened the back door of the car, he immediately jumped in. No hesitation, no fear. Which is exactly how Barney would have acted. But I still wasn't one-hundred-percent sure because there are a lot of big goldens in the world, and he wasn't acting like a dog would in a Disney movie if he was reunited with his owners after weeks apart. I went around to the driver's side, and when I got in, Linda was already turned around, hugging Barney's head and crying. I told her I thought it was Barney, but we couldn't be absolutely sure. Then she pointed to a scar on his front paw where the fur was a little thin, and I knew it was over. Barney had had a stubborn little sore place on his paw, and when it finally healed, the fur looked different. This distinctive marking meant it could only be him.

When we got him home and let him out of the car, his memory seemed to revive. He went around the perimeter of our yard, marking the territory, looked up and down the street, and then suddenly seemed to remember the doggie door I had made in our garage door. He went to it, sniffed, and nosed it, as if to make sure it was still available, then came back to where we were. It goes without saying that in the days ahead, Barney ate as well and received as much love and attention as any dog ever has.

I can't begin to describe what all this meant to me and Linda. However low we had been over losing Barney, we were that high or higher when we were reunited. We hugged and laughed and shed a tear or two, marveling over our bad luck and good luck, but through all this, Barney was just the same old Barney. One might think that he would fawn and slobber over us, be afraid of strangers, have PTSD, or need therapy, and the story might be better if he had. But he didn't. He had the same calm dignity and friendliness as always. And the same carnal appetites and playful wanderlust. And yes, we still let him run free. Immediately after his homecoming, we were a bit paranoid and more watchful than we had been before, but we ultimately decided that Barney was who he was, and forcing him into the mold of a house dog was not the right thing to do.

Although we never found out everything, we found out a lot about where in the world Barney had been. When we got home that first night, my first call was to the lady in Lynchburg. She had not given us a phone number, so we needed to find out how to contact the man who owned the house we had stolen/rekidnapped/rescued Barney from. During this call, she again referred to the reward. This had been a theoretical issue before, but now it was very much live, possibly involving the guy in Skippers, so I was probably a little cagey in talking about it with her.

I called the guy in Skippers later that night. He answered but had just returned home. I introduced myself and told him I was the guy who owned the dog he and his Lynchburg cousin had talked about. I still couldn't tell if he was aware of my conversation with her. I then told him I had taken Barney, but he apparently misunderstood what I was saying because he cautioned me against taking him and mentioned a shotgun. This wasn't said in a directly threatening way. As far as I can remember, his exact words were "Oh, anybody who tries to steal that dog is going to find himself on the other end of a shotgun." Maybe I should have been glad he loved Barney that much, but at the time I was a bit rattled. I clarified the fact that he was my dog and I had, in fact, *already* taken him. After I described the fence, etc., he went and looked and then understood. He seemed genuinely sad that Barney was gone. I suggested he call his cousin.

When I talked to him the next day, he seemed more resigned to losing Barney and said that although he would miss him, he was glad he got back home. I learned that he and his cousin had apparently worked out a deal on the reward, so that was out of the way. I then spent a long while talking about how he came to have Barney. Most of what is written below came from him.

There is a stone quarry near Skippers that is owned by Vulcan Materials and employed, in 1989, maybe twenty-five people. Near this quarry lived two women. I'm not sure exactly where, but they may have lived in a mobile home or RV. One day Barney happened to be foraging around the McDonald's, and they happened to be in Richmond eating at McDonald's, and for whatever reason, they kidnapped Barney. I'm sure he was happy to take whatever treat they offered and was even happy to get into their car (or RV or whatever). They took him back to Skippers, and he became their pet.

Now the story gets a little murky. At least some of the workmen at the quarry knew these women well enough to visit in their home, and there is some indication that the visits may have been commercial in nature. In any event, one or more of the workers took a liking to their beautiful dog. The women may have tired of Barney, or money may have changed hands, but one way or the other, Barney became the *quarry* pet. He lived at the quarry and was known and loved by everyone. Our source said they gave him a name, but I've forgotten what it was.

Whether he actually stayed at the quarry at night is unclear, but he was definitely the resident dog. Our source said he became a real favorite, not only of the people who worked there but of visitors, customers, etc., and related an example that occurred just after

Barney arrived at the quarry. I guess no one knew quite what to do with him, and when a truck driver from Roanoke, Virginia, said he sure would like to have him and could teach him to retrieve birds, his quarry friends said okay. Again, it isn't clear whether there was money involved. When the driver unloaded or finished his business, they looked for Barney and couldn't find him. They looked and called, but he seemed to be gone, and eventually the driver had to head back to Roanoke. Later Barney appeared from under some old truck covers. The men firmly believed he had been hiding because he liked it where he was and didn't want to go to Roanoke. Regardless of whether this was Barney's motivation, it solidified the men's determination to keep Barney with his new "family."

But then there came a time, apparently, when they thought someone needed to take responsibility for Barney. Our source was chosen for this, whether by lot, negotiation, or otherwise, so he ended up behind that fence where we found him. Linda and I often told each other how incredible it was that Barney navigated and survived everything that happened to him and ended up back with us. Granted, there were happenstances and bad luck involved in his disappearance, but there were far more instances of *good* luck in his recovery. What if we hadn't placed that additional ad? What if the Lynchburg lady hadn't read it? How did she connect the ad to a dog her cousin had mentioned to her? What if the women had just kept him? What if the guy from Roanoke had found him? What if we hadn't gone back to look one more time in Skippers? Good fortune indeed. Barney was meant to be back home.

Barney was a survivor in other ways too: He was hit by cars three times, late in life he was blind, until we got his cataracts taken off and new lenses put in, and he became diabetic when he was around thirteen. He was given up for dead, both by us and the vet, more than once but always made a comeback. When it finally came his time, at fifteen, we were both sad, but I have never seen a more heartbreaking separation than he from Linda and she from him. She rode with him in the back of our van on that last ride to the vet, and she held his big paw as he left us. From then on, and through our other canine friends, I marveled at how Linda's love and goodness was absorbed not just by humans. She designed a little micropark on our street with a whimsical bench painted like a Holstein cow and a plaque dedicating the place to Barney.

Linda received some letters from Barney after he died. He had his own letterhead, complete with a picture of him, listing as his residence "Richmond, Norfolk, Sandbridge," and the letters actually came via US mail. She thought they came from me, but if so, they were a forgery, since they were signed with a pawprint. Although she said they always made her cry, they were cheerful, and she looked forward to getting them. Here is a sample:

> Dear Mom,
>
> I was thinking the other day that it had been a long time since I wrote to you. I am still fine here, although at Christmas I sort of miss my real family. Say woof to Dad and my brothers.
>
> Someone who got here recently from Norfolk said you had a new furry friend there and that he was really cute and nice. I think she met him at a park just before she stopped running.[4] I am so happy you have him, and I know he and you and everyone will be happy. You are the best Mom a furry person could ever have.
>
> She also said she had seen a little park named after me. I couldn't believe it, but she described everything, and when I heard about the cow bench, I knew it could only be you. Thanks for remembering me. I still remember you.
>
> Love,
> Barney

---

4   Perhaps a reference to *Watership Down*, where "stopped running" was a synonym for "died."

16

Bodie

THE SECOND OF our Berners, Teddy, died in 2015. Predictably, it took us, particularly Linda, a while to recover, but recover we did, and Linda decided she wanted another golden, who she named Bodie.[5] He is a so-called English Cream variety and has no interest in chasing balls or anything else, so I tell people he's a pedigreed golden retriever and a wonderful friend, even if he isn't golden and won't retrieve.

We picked Bodie up from the breeder on a cold February day when he was ten weeks old or so. Despite the fact that he threw up in great volume on the way home, of course Linda and Bodie were completely in love from the beginning. Linda looked after housetraining, staying by his side almost constantly, even in the middle of the night, sensing when he needed to be carried outdoors for a rest stop, completing his lessons in tidiness within a few days. Bodie seemed to have an intense desire to please us, even more than the Berners did.

I don't really know what was in Bodie's head during and after Linda's illness, but I would catch him staring at her, sort of puzzled, and it was obvious he knew something was wrong. On the day she died, one of my sons said he looked like he was crying, and indeed he did. To this day, he seems to like blond women, and when I come

---

5 Why he was named Bodie is a story in itself. See chapter 44.

in from the garage, he often looks behind me, as if checking to see if she is there too. He is beside me as I write this, now *my* best friend but a constant reminder of Linda.

17

The Bighorn Sheepskin Co.

LINDA WAS ALWAYS LOOKING for the next new experience and new challenge. She had plenty to do, with managing our house and the beach house while dealing with three teenage boys, Spanish classes, belly dancing, etc., but she was restless for more. So in 1981 she decided to start her own business. We looked together at several possibilities, and she decided on the Bighorn Sheepskin Company. Bighorn was a well-known brand at that time, with two franchise models: One was a garden-variety storefront, and the other was a seasonal (i.e., Christmas) kiosk set up in a shopping mall. Linda chose the latter, as it allowed a sort of trial run without much of a lease or other commitment. The kiosk was a metal-frame enclosure that encouraged browsing during business hours and could be locked at night. The products were high-quality genuine sheepskin items, everything from slippers to vests to rugs. Very fuzzy, very inviting in cold weather, pretty expensive.

I may have aided and abetted this venture more than I should. I wanted it to be Linda's enterprise, for better or worse, wanted it to have weight, and wanted her to have a feeling of accomplishment. So, I set up a corporation for which I provided all the capital, but the stock of which was all owned by Linda and the boys. It was named B-Lark, using the initials from all our names. I ordered a briefcase with a B-Lark logo and "Linda Waddell, CEO" on it. Maybe a little over the top, but she liked it.

Linda was up very early and got home very late during that Christmas season. A daughter-in-law and I helped as best we could, but Linda took the brunt. The whole enterprise was very stressful on her, having to contend almost single-handedly with inventory, accounting, cashiering, shoplifting, and everything else that goes with retail.

It would be boring to get into B-Lark's P and L. It is enough to report that despite good sales and good management, it was more L than P. The initial investment was heftier than anticipated, with a cash register, supplies, the cost of shipping and returning the kiosk, etc., and you have to sell a whole lot of slippers to cover all that. Linda decided to hold a holiday clearance sale and call it a day with retail. I will admit to being relieved, but we always remembered Bighorn as being a ton of fun. I still have a pair of fuzzy slippers.

18

Road Atlanta

THIS MEMOIR IS way too short to contain the whole story of our experience with Road Atlanta, but it played too big a role to leave it out entirely. Road Atlanta is a 2.5-mile meandering road-style racetrack in Georgia that is very well-known in the sportscar racing industry. Through some unlikely circumstances, I and a couple of partners came to own the track in 1990, which turned out to be a financial disaster from an operating standpoint—but great fun.

Linda and I went to the track dozens of times, usually by train. It was an overnight sleeper, wonderfully timed. We boarded around dinnertime, turned in for a (sometimes) good sleep, and arrived in Gainesville, Georgia, the town where the track was, just in time to finish breakfast. One of my partners was actually the hands-on manager, so I seldom had to do anything but enjoy the races.

An outgrowth of the Road Atlanta years was the Paul Newman Ride, one of Linda's very favorite memories. Newman, you will recall, was a devoted sports car driver, and Road Atlanta was one of his favorite venues. He was often seen around the track and/or in town, and once in a while persuaded to take major sponsors around the track as a way of solidifying their support. Linda and I happened to be at the track on one of these occasions, and Linda ended up getting a few fast laps around the track in Paul's race car. She always described that ride as incredibly exciting, but the high point of her recollection was when he told her, "If you get really scared, just reach over and touch my shoulder." She said she relished the thrill of 125 mph on a curvy, unbanked track, but she sure would have liked to caress Paul Newman's shoulder.

Another Road Atlanta-related adventure came on a weekend when we were expecting a tremendous crowd. As it turned out, the crowd was less than tremendous, but all the owners (me included) had made elaborate preparations for miles of traffic gridlock. Extra parking, extra police presence, traffic controls, etc. Linda and I made our own special preparations, one of which was to rent an RV so we could arrive before the traffic, stay at the track for a couple of days, and leave after the jam, thus avoiding the need to get in and out to a hotel. Unfortunately, we made some mistakes in executing this plan.

There were just the two of us, but I wanted to be comfortable, so I made Mistake No. 2 (No. 1 was the whole harebrained idea in the first place), which was to get a Big RV. Really Big. Over forty feet long. Nice big beds, a nice sitting area, and a spacious kitchen and bath. Mistake No. 3 was thinking I could drive the thing. I had driven a twenty-foot U-Haul truck and figured it couldn't be that much different, but it was. We finally made it to the track, but it became clear that we didn't really have a decent place to park this beast. We had RV spaces, but not near the track offices and tower overlooking the track, which is where we liked to hang out. We eventually found a spot, but it wasn't level, which revealed Mistake No. 4.

As noted, I had sprung for a Big RV, but to save money, I hadn't paid much attention to how modern it was or what niceties it had. One of the niceties that you need in an RV, *especially* if you're an amateur taking it to a primitive location, is an auto-leveling system, or at least the equipment to level it manually. Linda and I didn't even know the thing *had* to be level, much less how to do it. We soon learned. We were unlevel front to back *and* side to side. The water wouldn't work, the toilet wouldn't flush, and we could tell that a tilting bed wouldn't allow any meaningful sleep. There ensued an afternoon of scouting up concrete blocks, two-by-eights, and a ton of trial and error driving up on those crude supports. We never got it right, but we got close enough to give up.

Mistake No. 5 was in not realizing that we needed a way to dispose of wastewater: either a sewer hookup (not available, since we were in a made-up space) or a honey wagon, a vehicle that makes the rounds in an RV park and receives wastewater. By the time the weekend events were over and we were ready to leave the track, however, virtually all other RVs had left and the honey wagon was nowhere to be seen. As an owner of the track, I suppose I could have found it and ordered it up, but it seemed much simpler to just find a place to drain the tank. So I drove off the jerry-rigged levelers, found a more or less deserted place in the infield, and let it fly. I never told even my partners about that one, and I'm not very proud of it, but maybe there was a lot of rain that week.

19

John Michael

LINDA HAD A SERIOUS boyfriend in high school, continuing, at least on and off, into college years, but nonetheless I think I was the love of Linda's life. Aside, that is, from John Michael Montgomery. She was hopelessly and irrevocably in love with John Michael from about 1994 until late in her life, maybe until she died. She made no secret of it, and I came to accept, and be resigned to, my secondary status.

John Michael was a country singer with a relatively brief but meteoric career. He was from Nicholasville, Kentucky, not far from Lexington, and had some very big hits in the '90s. It is fair to say that he was among the very top country artists during that time. He was equally at home with rock or love songs and had to his credit Songs of the Year, Grammys, etc. And was and is, apparently, a nice guy to boot.

The decade of the 1990s, when his career was peaking, was also the decade of our Road Atlanta days. One of the ventures we cooked up at Road Atlanta was an outdoor country music concert, dubbed the First Annual Georgia Country Music Festival, a two-day affair in May 1994, featuring some of the biggest names of the day.[6] Our headliner was Billy Ray Cyrus, whose "Achy Breaky Heart" was a humongous hit that catapulted him to near-Elvis status for a year or so (although he is

---

6   This was, incidentally, the event that prompted the Big RV fiasco.

now perhaps better remembered as Miley's dad). But there were other big names as well, like Delbert McClinton and Mark Wills.

In addition, there were three very well-known but not-yet-quite-top-rank performers: Legend has it that two of them, Faith Hill and Tim McGraw, actually met and/or fell in love that weekend at Road Atlanta. And it is fact, not just legend, that native Americans noisily picketed and protested McGraw's performance because of his song "Indian Outlaw."

The third up-and-comer was John Michael Mongomery. When we put the festival together, a year or so in advance, he was a very successful singer, but by the time May 1994 arrived, he had also arrived, in a big way. His hit song "I Swear" had just won Song of the Year. Linda fell in love. In fact, she fell before that weekend, so when he arrived at Road Atlanta, she was ready to meet him, talk to him, and get his autograph on a JMM T-shirt she had just purchased and was wearing. She described that signing in the most enthusiastic and tactile terms.

John Michael performed that evening on an elevated stage in front of thousands (not as many thousands as we had hoped, but still thousands) of screaming fans. There was a fence barrier between the performers and the audience, but we arranged to get through it for his performance, so we were as close as it was possible to get, unless you were part of the show. Linda was thrilled beyond words.

She continued to be a passionate fan through his peak years in the 1990s. She even ordered one of those stand-up cardboard figures for our family room as an over-the-top joke to show friends. Perhaps her most fervent JMM venture, though, was to a benefit concert he gave in Nicholasville, Kentucky, for the private school where his child was enrolled (or maybe the child of a close friend or relative—I don't remember). The concert was supposed to be a strictly closed affair, just for parents, staff, and donors. However, a good friend of ours had a child at the school, and somehow Linda found out about the concert and wrangled an invitation.

Now, Nicholasville is not an easy place to get to from Norfolk, Virginia, so Linda arranged for our youngest son, who flew his own plane, to take her to Nicholasville and back for this event. Off they went to the concert, and she reported later that it was a great time. She even got John Michael's guitar pick. Linda continued to follow his career over the thirty years after Road Atlanta. He announced his retirement in 2024. I'll bet Linda would have sent him a note.

2 0

Motorcycles and Other Gifts

OVER THE YEARS, as you might expect, there were lots and lots of gifts between us, some conventional and some not so much so. But there were three gifts that fell into the category of Things That Seemed Like Good Ideas at the Time.

The first was pecuniary. Linda never had much interest in things financial. It wasn't so much that she didn't know much about money and investments as it was that she just left that to me. It was part of our division of duties. But about the time I was closing in on sixty, in the 1990s, I was becoming more aware of my mortality and thought it would be good if Linda had a better awareness of, and involvement in, our investments. When there came an opportunity to transfer a block of stock I was about to receive in a merger, I figured it could serve as the foundation of an investment portfolio that she could manage and play with and learn something from, even though it wasn't a lot of money. We opened an account in her sole name at a local broker, which became known between us as Linda's Fortune.

In the end, though, the nuances of stocks and bonds, dividend reinvestment plans, etc., weren't her thing. She was content to watch, wait, and hold, not really being interested in tending the garden. But she loved the fact that her Fortune was there, provided in her will that it go to her siblings and to a dear friend, and took great pleasure in knowing that's what would happen.

The second gift in this category arose from the fact that during their younger teenage years, the three boys and I rode motorcycles (dirt bikes, that is, although mine was street legal, and I occasionally took it on quieter city streets or country roads) almost every weekend. We had our favorite places, like the woods and power line easement that ran close to our house, so on many weekends, we would strap on little coolers of drinks and head out, all four of us.

Between these expeditions and all the maintenance, etc., we were spending a lot of time away from home. Linda loved the fact that the boys and I had found this commonality, and she never complained about being left behind. In fact, she usually helped in the preparations and was there to greet us when we came back and told her of that day's adventures (we left out the misadventures, unless a cut or scrape gave us away) on the trails.

But still, sometimes we thought we were making her kind of a dirt bike widow, akin to a golf widow but less classy. So, when her birthday rolled around, the boys and I considered flowers or dinner but eventually decided on the very tender and romantic gesture of getting her a motorcycle so she could be in the gang. We toyed with getting a real dirt bike but decided she might not really be ready for that, so we decided on a Vespa-like motor scooter, figuring that if it all worked out, maybe she would later want to graduate to something more muscular.

I found such a thing, used but running, and we lovingly presented it to her. Linda said it was *such* a neat thing to do, *such* an exciting thing, that she couldn't wait to try it out. Whether, as I look back on it, this was grace and politeness on her part or in fact willingness and eagerness to try something new, I don't know, but in any case, at the first opportunity, we set out together, five bikes in a row, for a trail and dirt road adventure. Needless to say, it didn't end well. We, the boys and I, had gotten used to ruts, mud, roots, and rocks and hadn't been nearly realistic enough about the suitability of a tiny engine, low frame, and small tires. Linda gamely tried to join in the fun and keep up, but it eventually became clear that she was doing more bogging down than riding, and we were doing more lifting and heaving than enjoying. We kept that vehicle for a time, and Linda rode it to and from the grocery store and other places close by, but the hoped-for gang expansion from four to five never got off the ground.

Now one would think there was a lesson learned there: *Don't buy your wife a present that's more your thing than hers.* One would think. But somehow this got by me, which led to the third gift. When I was maybe forty-five, I took up hunting and began spending more and more time in the fields and forests. I decided Linda and I could have some additional together time if I included her. The kind of hunting I did was pretty amateur. I just took my shotgun, went out to some place (public or private) where hunting was permitted, and walked around, hoping for game birds or squirrels or whatever. Linda could join me on these jaunts without any equipment, license, or expertise. We went a couple of Saturdays, and had a good time, but I could tell she found it a little boring, or felt like a fifth wheel, so I decided to surprise her and truly include her in the sport. You guessed it: I thought about flowers and candy and love notes, but instead I bought her a twenty-gauge Mossberg shotgun, complete with a nice case and boxes of shells.

She was only slightly less enthusiastic about the gun than she had been about the Vespa, and again I don't really know whether it was real or synthetic. But in any case, the next weekend we set off for the hunting grounds. It was kind of exciting for both of us, partners in the hunt, ready to slay dangerous beasts like quail or rabbits. The only thing I remember about that first hunt is that Linda tried to shoot me. We were walking along in an open field, with me in front looking for targets and her twenty or thirty yards to my right and a little behind. As often happens in bird hunts, suddenly a covey of something (I assume quail or grouse) rose into the air in front of us, wings beating and leaves rattling. I was raising my gun to have a shot when I felt something whiz past my ear, proving two things:

One, Linda was quicker on the draw than I was, and two, I should have ducked. We were more careful in our walking formation after that. This was many years before Dick Cheney famously shot his hunting companion in Texas, but when I saw that story, I understood immediately what had happened.

The whole hunting togetherness attempt was basically a flop, and I altogether gave up hunting shortly thereafter. I guess the only profit was that Linda actually shot that shotgun a few times and learned a little about firearms in the process.

So there you have it: three gifts that were, at least in retrospect, ill-advised but remind me one more time of what an extraordinarily layered and rich person Linda was.

2 1

Two Hips and a Back

BEGINNING WHEN SHE was barely forty, Linda was plagued with arthritis in her neck and back. At first it was just an annoyance, managed with Advil or something, but it kept getting worse, first interfering with tennis and then with everyday activities. She was not a complainer, in fact just the opposite, so she tried to play through it for several years, with hot compresses and the like. But finally she got a full exam and found out she had a seriously deteriorating neck and spine. After that, it was several years of physical therapy, injections, and heavier medication (although never real narcotics). Still, Linda resisted giving up tennis or other activities.

Then she began having serious trouble with her left hip. She attributed it to an incident that happened on a walk with one of our big Bernese mountain dogs. He apparently pulled suddenly in a direction she wasn't prepared for, she felt a sharp pain, and she couldn't put her full weight on that side. We kept waiting for it to improve, but it never really did.

By that time, her back was in serious trouble. Virtually constant pain, inability to do ordinary tasks, certainly no athletics. She began looking at the possibility of surgery. Her sister, Judy, had had very successful back and neck surgery a few years earlier. We went to Florida to visit with Judy's surgeon, and investigated other possibilities as well. Linda finally settled on a renowned spinal surgeon at Johns Hopkins in Baltimore, and we began preparations. I can't say she was eager for the operation, but she wasn't afraid of it either. The prospect of being free of her chronic misery was certainly a motivating force, and we thought, and the surgeon thought, the extensive back repair might help her hip as well.

Extensive is not a strong enough word for the surgery. She was on the table for almost eight hours, and the incision in her back went from just below her neck to just above her coccyx. Especially for a woman in her seventies, it was an incredibly stressful—not to mention dangerous—procedure, but it was largely successful. She spent a week-plus at Johns Hopkins and another week-plus at a rehab hospital in Baltimore. In both places, I slept in her room most nights. It's hard to be happy in a hospital, still in pain, but we made the best of it. We talked and read, and sometimes I would go out for late-night ice cream, rushing back to her room before it melted. Gradually, she improved, and after that long two weeks, I was able to bring her home, in a wheelchair. Now began months of physical therapy in Norfolk, and eventually she recovered entirely from the spinal repair.

Unfortunately, the problem with her left hip was unimproved, despite the therapists' focus on it and their best efforts. So, we began looking into the possibility of surgery on the hip itself. It was a challenge. Without getting into the intricacies of hip structure, suffice it to say that her particular injury was not something surgeons in the Norfolk area were willing to get into. They said the success rate was so low that they couldn't recommend it. Unwilling to give up, we consulted with a hip specialist (also renowned) at Johns Hopkins, and he was willing to try the repair, so back we went. This surgery was not as extensive as the back operation, and after a brief stay, I brought Linda back to Norfolk and began more PT. No real improvement occurred, and imaging showed the repair had not held.

Still unwilling to give up, Linda asked the Hopkins surgeon if there was anything else to be done and was told there was a small chance that a different technique might have a better result. Another trip to Hopkins, another surgery, more PT, but no better result. She had a routine hip replacement on her right hip a little later, a procedure that gave her no trouble at all, but the left never really improved.

So, finally, Linda had to give in to the reality of a permanent limp and a cane. This was perhaps the bitterest pill she had ever had to swallow, but it didn't, in the end, diminish her beauty, charm, sunny outlook, genuineness, or capacity for love. We went to Jamaica, Big Sur, my class reunion in Fort Thomas, and a variety of other places, all with a limp and a cane. As far as I could ever tell, her life-changing struggles with these physical problems never gave rise to regret, resentment, or depression about her lot in life. I am only now realizing how extraordinary this was.

Just Plain Fun

If Marilyn Can Do It . . .

Love at First Sight, Somewhere in Europe

Barney at Sandbridge Beach

You Wash, I'll Dry

A Fifteen-Year Love Affair

Surfing with Andy, 2005

Linda at Sandbridge Beach, 1990

The Ride of Her Life: Paul Newman at Road Atlanta

Bodie

PART IV
Places

WE WERE LUCKY enough to travel a lot during our years together. The fact that we got to see more places than the average bears wasn't because we were jet setters. My doings and career took me on trips all over the US (and, less often, all over the world), and because I enjoyed traveling more with Linda than without, she often went with me. Not only did we see a lot and do a lot, but the getting there and getting around were a part of the fun. Planes, trains, helicopters, boats, buses, automobiles, dog sleds, camels, tuk-tuks, and rickshaws each created a kind of intimate memory. This part is about a few of those memories.

2 2

Travels

SOMETIMES THE PLACES we went, how we got there, and what we did were selected and planned by us, and sometimes they were built around meetings or business. We went to really neat places, like St. Martin, Maui, China, or Svalbard, but also to more business-y places like Hong Kong or London. Sometimes our destinations were places we had been before, so they felt like old hangouts, but more often they were new, so there was the excitement of new scenery, customs, languages. Always, though, it was really the *sharing* that mattered.

But there were three significant exceptions to the sharing rule. She took two European jaunts with her dearest friends (more later), some train escapes to Florida that I arranged and sprang on her (also more later), and an impulsive stay in Switzerland. The latter occurred at the end of a business trip to Zurich. We had arranged to drive down through the beautiful Swiss Alps to Lucerne for a few days. It was charming, so much so that Linda just couldn't bear to leave. Since I *had* to go home for business reasons, we arranged an additional week for her in Lucerne, in a little hotel right near that beautiful, flowered bridge that is the city's trademark. I will admit to being a little apprehensive, since a single woman in a foreign country (at least in those days) inherently gave rise to a bit of apprehension and since Linda's international travel had always been with me. But my worry was for nothing, as you might guess. She had a wonderful time, met interesting people, enjoyed the city, and rode lots of trains to the surrounding area.

It would be really hard to pick our Best Trip, but one of the contenders would be our first trans-Pacific trip, which included Hong Kong, Thailand, India, and (briefly) Cambodia and Japan. I had a business trip that took me to Hong Kong, which was an experience all its own, particularly our side trips to Kowloon and some other islands, but the bulk of the trip was spent in India and Thailand.

I had a longtime classmate and friend who was with the CIA in New Delhi, although he was thinly disguised as a US State Department employee. Somehow, he found out we were going to be in Asia and invited us to visit with him and his wife. We had an incredible time there, being squired around by State Department drivers and staying in their beautiful home. We saw sites like the Taj Mahal but also places tourists seldom go. Linda and I both came home with a variety of kurta pajamas and other Indian apparel, which came in handy when one of our sons married a girl of Indian extraction (more later).

My friend's previous post, before India, was Bangkok. Either because of that or just because we thought Thailand was fascinating, we also spent several days there. We hired local guides who turned out to be honest, knowledgeable, friendly, and fun to be with. In addition to showing us where to buy the best fake Rolex watches, they took us in a motorboat up some river to an open-air market on the Cambodian border. A photo captured the highlight of that little excursion, Linda with a hundred-pound python draped around her neck.

The other trip that would be in the running for Best is Norway. We had been to Oslo and its immediate environs a few years earlier for a weekend business meeting, but this second trip (around 2014, I think) was purely for pleasure, arranged because we wanted to see the midnight sun, a phenomenon visible only from above the Arctic Circle. There are a number of accessible places where this is possible, including some in Alaska, but we chose Tromso, Norway, partly because we had been charmed by Norway on the first trip. Tromso is a town of 70,000 or so in northern Norway, big enough to be quite civilized, with commercial air service, but by no means is it a tourist destination. We thought it would be fun to poke around other parts of Norway on the way there, so we flew into Bergen, near the southern tip of the country, and took a Hurtigruten ship up the coast to Tromso.

Hurtigruten is a cruise line, and its ships are quite luxurious, but since it stops at a lot of towns and you can arrange to get on and off at will, Norwegians sometimes use it simply as transportation. In any case, it was very comfortable. We went in and out of many scenic inlets and fjords, eventually crossing the Arctic Circle. That crossing gives rise to a celebration, sort of like crossing the equator. If it's a clear night, the sun, sure enough, dips toward the horizon, but then it starts back up. It's not bright sun, but enough to cast shadows, and the whole effect is enchanting. Linda and I hugged and drank a glass of whatever was being served, but we didn't last much longer, it being midnight and we being old people, as they say.

A day or two later we docked in Tromso, which was as charming as we had hoped. Among other things, we went to our first European soccer game. This was a very local experience, and since neither of us actually knew the sport or even the rules, we probably stuck out like American sore thumbs. But we had fun. There were churches to see, shops to visit, and good restaurants with legitimately Norwegian food.

After a few days exploring Tromso, we began looking at side trips. We had another few days before we were scheduled to fly out, and Tromso was a perfectly nice place to spend them, but a flyer advertising an expedition even further north caught our eye, and we decided to try it.

We were almost at the northern tip of Norway, but if you go directly north from there, literally halfway to the North Pole, you get to the Svalbard archipelago, a territory of Norway. We flew in on a plane that was a lot like an old DC-3, chewing gum and all. Much of the archipelago is barren, but there is a town, Longyearbyen, which has an airport, a motel, and places to eat, the northernmost town on Earth of more than 1,000 residents. Originally a mining town, it is now trying to take advantage of its climate and location: it is home to a facility that studies the Northern Lights and the Svalbard Global Seed Vault, containing millions of different kinds of seeds, frozen and preserved, just in case of a world cataclysm. Its website says it holds the most diverse collection of food crop seeds in the world. I wanted to visit the Seed Vault, figuring it was something not everyone had on their résumé, but Linda couldn't get up much enthusiasm for it.

We were there in late July, but it was as cold as its location implies. The second day was colder than the first, and when it snowed, we decided to take a ride in a real dog sled. Inexplicably, since I was seventy-plus and not in great shape, I was selected, from the dozen or so people who came for the ride, to get the dogs from the dog yard and drive the sled. The dogs, each tied to a stake, were *very* excited, barking and yapping and straining at their chains, and I was not very enthusiastic when the guy told me to grab one by the collar, unhook his chain, and take him over to the sled. I was convinced, by their behavior, that these were untamed or even vicious beasts who would sense immediately that I was not even an Average Dog, let alone a Top Dog, and would want me for lunch. To my surprise, however, they were just dogs, with the standard affection for humans. Their excitement was not at the prospect of taking a bite out of me; it was simply because they wanted to pull the sled. That's what they were born and bred for, and they were ecstatic to be hooked up and told to mush (actually, there was a word they gave me to make them go, but I've forgotten what it was).

Linda thought all this was hilarious. For years, she kidded me about the look on my face as I approached the dog yard and the lack of authority in my commands until I found my confidence as a musher. It was for sure one of our favorite trips.

There were other great trips. Runners-up would have to include the train/air trip to Churchill, Manitoba, to spend several days with polar bears, the European vacation (yes, a lot like the movie) we took with the kids, and the river cruise on the Yangtze River in China. I recently counted up and found we had been together to almost all the fifty states and forty-one foreign countries. We didn't keep a perfect pictorial record but enough to give us hours of pleasure looking back. Linda, always photogenic, makes some of the photos great all by herself. I find myself choosing pics that she is in, partly because they remind me of our experiences, but mostly because I treasure her smile in those new places.

23

Trains, Long and Short

THE FIRST TIME trains became a part of our life was in 1961, while I was still at Williams College. Linda was working for the old Pennsylvania Railroad in Cincinnati, and in those days, there was a direct train from Cincinnati to New York City, which, as an employee, Linda got to ride free. Williams isn't that far from New York City, so we hatched a plan to meet there. It was a wonderful couple of days. Linda had never been to New York, so we hit all the tourist destinations, including the Statue of Liberty. Unfortunately, we didn't pay attention to the returning ferry schedule from the statue, and Linda ended up missing her train home, so we had to stay an extra day. Since we were essentially penniless, we had to figure out how to score a hotel room without paying for it, but that's another story. Predictably, Linda's excuse as to why she wasn't at work the next day (true as it was) was met with some skepticism at the PRR in Cincinnati.

It was in New York City on that very trip that I asked Linda to marry me. I am going to say I was on bended knee and that it was atop the Empire State Building. It may not have been, or maybe it was, or it should have been. I gave her an actual diamond ring (a small one), the down payment on which took a good chunk of my summer earnings, and I think Linda was genuinely surprised. She said yes. I knew I was happy about that, but at twenty-one, I probably didn't realize how life-changing and lasting our bond would be.

We rode trains every chance we got, here and in Europe, Asia, Africa, and South America. We made several trips across the United States and Canada, two of which were with the kids and were very family-oriented. Each of the kids had his own roomette, and Linda and I had a larger bedroom. We would be together for meals (three daily), poke around the lounge or observation cars during the day, and play cards or board games in one of our compartments in the evening.

Trips without kids (there were two of those across the country as well) were more leisurely, but they were still exciting and romantic and relaxing all at once. Occasionally, the train would stop for a while, I guess to take on water or something. For some reason, two of these stops, on two different trips, stand out in my memory.

The first was in New Mexico (Albuquerque, I think), where the train was greeted by a huge display of Native American goods, including jewelry, crafts, apparel, historical information, etc. It was torridly hot, but I managed to surreptitiously buy a pair of turquoise earrings configured as bear claws. I gave them to Linda for Christmas. When she opened them, she said she vividly recalled the stop, and couldn't believe I had braved that heat just to shop for something for her.

The other stop was in Salt Lake City, where, on westbound trips, the train split into two trains, one bound for Los Angeles and the other for San Francisco. It was dusk, and from the front of the station, off in the distance, one could see the incredibly dramatic spires of the Mormon Tabernacle, with its lights just coming on, a unique and unforgettable view. When we returned to the platform, we watched the switch engines separate and rearrange cars into two trains and noticed a man placing pennies on the track right under the wheels of one of the cars. When we asked him why, he said when the train moved, the pennies would be flattened and make nice souvenirs. It was one of the few places in the Amtrak system, he said, where a passenger could do this, since normally passengers would be on board when the train moved. Naturally, we scared up some pennies, and each of our kids created a souvenir. They may still have them.

When we rode trains, we sat, talked, held hands, read the information about the train route that we always brought, met interesting people in the dining car, and learned to sleep reasonably well in a lurching sleeper. I recommend it.

You've probably heard of cruises to nowhere. One time we arranged a train trip to nowhere, an afternoon/evening trip via rail from Norfolk to Richmond and back with a dozen or so friends. Cocktails and hors d'oeuvres on the way up, dinner at a place near the Richmond train station, and Bailey's and brandy on the way back. People still talk about that trip. Perhaps someday I'll do it again.

Maybe the most fun train adventures were trips the boys and I arranged as a surprise. It was probably in the mid-eighties. Linda and I, but particularly Linda, were feeling pressure about some teenage boy issues, and I was afraid she might be getting depressed or overwhelmed. Besides that, it was cold in Richmond, and Linda hated winter and cold weather, to the point that I actually wondered, sometimes, whether she suffered from seasonal affective disorder (SAD).

So, I decided to give her a little vacation. Just her, by herself. The boys and I talked it over and decided to try to make it as much of a surprise as we could, so we worked out a plan that would keep it secret as long as possible. We decided Sawgrass, not far from St. Augustine, Florida, was a good destination. Not too far, but almost certain to have moderate weather. There was an overnight train directly from Richmond to near Sawgrass, with an ideal dinner-to-breakfast schedule, so I arranged as luxurious a sleeper as they had, booked a rental car, found a resort hotel on the beach, and packaged up all the information (with some cash, important in those days) in a sealed envelope.

We had to tell Linda she was going on a trip, someplace warm, so she could pack, but that's all we told her. The boys and I drove her over to the train station, and when the train came, I found the conductor, let him in on the deal, and gave him the envelope, making him promise he wouldn't give it to Linda until the next morning. The plan was that he would wake her up in sunny Florida and she would find out where she was going to spend a few days in pampered luxury. In fact, it all went just as intended. Not everyone would have been adventurous enough to enjoy all the unknowns, but Linda was, and she did. She came back after a week refreshed and revitalized. It was all such a success that I sent her two other times on Florida train vacations, those times without all the elaborate secrecy.

The last train trip I will note was perhaps the most memorable of all, in South Africa on a luxury line called Rovos Rail. I had a business meeting there, and we extended it to include a wonderful ride over several days through a large part of South Africa. Our accommodations took up half a modern train car, complete with a king-size bed, large parlor area, full-sized bathtub, shower, etc. Days were spent either enjoying the scenery and wildlife or taking mini safaris by jeep. The train stopped overnight, so sleeping was bliss.

One of the countries Rovos Rail passed through was the Kingdom of Swaziland (now Eswatini). We stopped for some very exotic food and souvenirs and learned of a current political/social kerfuffle that had the local population stirred up. It seemed that the king had recently chosen a young girl (I don't remember exactly how young, but I think fifteen-ish) to join his several existing wives. This was viewed as either a great honor, very traditional, and very welcomed by the girl and her family or as a backward, anti-feminist, and abusive practice not to be tolerated. The impression we got was that the local populace mostly took the former view and wished the vocal advocates of the latter view (including a lot of Europeans) would mind their own damn business. Linda and I were of different opinions, so we decided to ignore the fuss and enjoy the rest of the ride.

24

And . . . Cabooses

LINDA AND I were always looking for offbeat things to do. We enjoyed the usual—good weather and elegant surroundings—but also liked new, unusual adventures. One weekend (a holiday, I think) we decided to combine this love of the unusual with our love of trains and go camping in a caboose. As I recall, it was out in the middle of nowhere, with a few other old cabooses scattered around and plenty of room for additional camping, a fire, etc. Very private, but with all the amenities of . . . a caboose: toilet facilities (sort of), running water (as long as you didn't use too much), a hot plate, refrigerator, potbellied stove, and bunk beds. We had one of the 125-pound Berners (I think it was Teddy) with us, so things were pretty cozy. Teddy was accustomed to sleeping in our bed, so he tried to get in a bunk with one of us, but the bunks were way too small for that.

Neither of us knew much about living in primitive quarters, let alone camping, so we were making it up as we went along. We wondered aloud whether train crews could really be comfortable in these things. Nevertheless, we had a great time (although, to be honest, we probably wouldn't have wanted more than a couple of days), walking in the woods, chatting with some of the other residents (some had been in the cabooses many times), reading, or just talking. As much as anything else, we noticed and enjoyed the quiet. I remember telling Linda around a fire that I had a kind of different, almost-mystical feeling out there, with the fire, the quiet, the isolation, and the big (bigger than it looks at a distance) presence of the caboose. We talked about where that caboose might have been. Maybe on the same tracks we had travelled?

2 5

Boats: RMS[7] Queen Mary 2

I DON'T REMEMBER why we chose 2007 for this expedition. I had turned sixty-five recently, and although I hadn't really retired, I had some money coming, so I think maybe that had something to do with it. In any case, we decided to blow the money (and some more) on an all-family, all-inclusive cruise to England, including an outgoing voyage on the newest Cunard Lines steamer, the Queen Mary 2. Seven days on the QM2, a few days in London and environs, and a flight back to the States, all with three sons, three significant others, and a grandson, two and a half. Recounting this adventure in any kind of detail would take a long time. The gist is that it provided a lot of family togetherness, in a way we hadn't had before, partly because we didn't live close together. We had nice accommodations for the kids but sprang for the nicest for ourselves: a sitting room, separate bedroom, and big balcony, enough space to use as a gathering place for the whole clan.

I ordered a bunch of gear for the occasion and needed a logo or motto. The trip was costing more money than I had ever before spent in one place on frivolity, and that money was, in some sense, family money, so I decided to confront this fact head-on. I had golf shirts, duffel bags, mugs, and a variety of other mementoes

---

7   For a bit of fun, try to guess what this prefix stands for.

embroidered or inscribed with "*Hilaritas Vitae Superare Hereditas*," which I believed to be Latin for "having fun in life is more important than an inheritance." Latin scholars may tell me it translates to "eat a jelly donut," but you get the idea.

Transatlantic trips on Cunard, at least in those days, were pretty formal. At dinner, coats and ties for the men and gowns for the ladies. Some men appeared for dinner in black tie throughout the trip, but we decided to go for this only on one night. Partly, this was in the interests of not having to bring formal wear with us (it could be rented on the ship) and partly in the interests of not having to fool with it every night. On the night we *did* get gussied up, we had a photo taken, and the kids presented us a canvas print of it at the end of the trip. That wonderful print still hangs over my fireplace.

But there was casual fun as well. We had provided some shipboard credit for everyone, so there were spa treatments and other luxuries galore, and every night, either before or after dinner, there were shows to see and bands to dance to. Speaking of which, Waddell men don't dance, as a rule. I don't know exactly why; we just don't. But on the QM2, this rule didn't hold true. All of us, perhaps to our surprise, danced fast and slow. One night, maybe the one when we were all dressed up, one of the significant others said she had seen us dancing and asked how we had stayed so much in love for forty-five years. I don't remember what we said, but I remember thinking how true it was, how glad I was she had noticed. If we hadn't been in love already, I think we would have fallen in love on the QM2.

One of the biggest hits of the voyage was young grandson Tommy. For dinner, he was dressed up in a manner that was as near formal as it gets for a toddler. One outfit in particular, a sailor suit, complete with a yachting cap, provoked requests for photo ops from about everyone. One of the very best mementos of that trip is a picture of Tommy being held by the commodore commanding the ship.

But the thing that most sticks in my mind is how much Linda and I enjoyed each other on that trip. We had some heartfelt talks with our companions about what forty-five years of marriage meant, and we shared some stories they probably hadn't heard before. But the best moments were after the evenings wore down, when we would sit on that balcony, usually just the two of us, and talk about the day, the ship, or just how lucky we were. There's nothing quite like a moonlit ocean to summon up stuff like that.

26

Somerset, Kentucky

THIS TOWN PLAYED such an influential role in Linda's life that it isn't just a place; it needs a mention of its own. Somerset is a town of 10,000 or so, located an hour south of Lexington, just on the edge of the Appalachian Mountains. Linda's parents were from there and married there, and Linda was born there. Although they moved to Northern Kentucky after a few years, Somerset was always, in a sense, Home. Linda's dad was adopted, so she knew nothing about his biological family, but her mom grew up on a farm (as in no electricity, no indoor plumbing), and Linda had a ton of memories about that farm, both from her very early years and the many visits later on. Although Linda spent most of her formative years in suburbia, she talked a lot about her "country" roots. She kept close ties to the many relatives there. Linda and I visited a couple of times before we were married, and she took our kids there on spring and summer vacations. The Somerset connection was made stronger by the fact that several of Linda's aunts (her mom's sisters) also moved to Northern Kentucky. In due course, this led to a bunch of cousins near Linda's age, which deepened (albeit indirectly) the Somerset connection.

We attended many family reunions in Somerset over the years. A reunion of her family consists of a Saturday afternoon in a big tent erected on her Uncle Darwin's farm. There are games for kids and adults, a rowboat if anyone wants to go out on the pond, a ton of kinfolks (usually including some who have never met each other), and a ton of food. Maybe a ton and a half. One year we took Andy the Berner to this event, rented a conversion van so he would have room to move around, and drove from Norfolk to Somerset. He was the hit of the party, with a couple of major qualifications. He was beautiful, friendly, and generally well-behaved, but the fried chicken and hot dogs drove him crazy, so you had to keep an eye out. We were reminded that dogs are not always looked at the same way in rural America as they are in the suburbs. On farms, especially among older generations, they are often regarded more as working animals, not necessarily even being allowed indoors, so he was not universally welcomed.

I still go to these reunions and am treated as graciously as if I were blood.

Linda's parents are both gone now. They moved back to Somerset for the last decade or so of their lives. Every time we visited with them, they seemed very happy to be Home.

27

Big Sur

IF "ALWAYS ON MY MIND" was Our Song, Big Sur, California, was Our Place. It's lots of people's favorite place, of course, but to us it was something truly magical: at once a fun, quirky place, a place of casual elegance, and an explosion of natural beauty and grandeur, an unequaled combination of meditative quiet, sumptuous scenery, and sometimes a throwback vibe. It is its own land, one we never tired of, one we always went back to, no matter how many times we had been.

Big Sur has no specific boundaries. It's generally thought to include the area along the California coast from Carmel on the north to Cambria/San Simeon on the south, a distance of a hundred miles or so. There is a post office in a tiny town that is officially Big Sur, but often the name is used to include the whole area. It's a very unusual mixture of old and avant-garde, historical and modern, and is the subject of a continual battle to preserve natural beauty. There are luxurious spots like Ventana and Post Ranch Inn, where you can pay $2,500 per night and find food and wine absolutely second to none, but for the most part, the shops, restaurants, and places to stay are modest, sometimes even rugged.

Part of the charm is the weather. We were usually there in the dead of summer. Even then, it wasn't unusual to wake up to fifties and fog dense, enough to convince you that it was going to be a miserable day. Later in the morning, though, the fog usually begins to burn off, leaving spectacular rolling fog banks out over the ocean, and the sun comes out and it's seventy. At sundown, of course, it's the reverse, so the Big Sur experience involves figuring out when to take clothing layers on and off.

The road that runs through Big Sur, California Highway One, is an engineering marvel of its own. In recent years, particularly, it has been difficult to keep open. Mudslides created by heavy rainstorms sometimes make large areas of Big Sur inaccessible by car, and the blockages can last for months, even a year or more. Residents and businesses have to get accustomed to having access only from the north or only from the south. Worst of all, of course, are multiple closures, when those between the closures have to find emergency transport, be it by boat, helicopter, or otherwise. Those of us who love to visit there have learned to check carefully, in advance, as to what parts of the highway are open.

The flavor and ambiance of Big Sur, which is very hard to convey, is revealed to some extent by those who lived there or made it a hangout. People like William Randolph Hearst (of Hearst Castle and *Citizen Kane* fame), Jack Kerouac ("beatnik" and author of *Big Sur*, an autobiographical novel), Henry Miller, Orson Welles, and Rita Hayworth, all of whom lived there for a while. In the 1960s, perhaps inspired by its increasing notoriety or by an accepting and untraditional vibe, "hippies" arrived in Big Sur in large numbers. One can still distinctly feel that sixties influence today.

Linda and I, over the years, came to have favorite places and returned to them trip after trip: gift shops with local crafts, places to eat, places to sleep, and places just to sit and look at the gorgeous coastline where mountains meet the sea in a riot of rocks and surf. When I miss Linda, which is every day, the special things I think about include the many times in Big Sur when we melted into the surroundings and each other. Two people can share interests, whether musical or philosophical, come together in those things, and share each other's feelings, but to us there was something about

Big Sur, and its majesty yet quietude, that is unique. The moments and hours we spent there were enchanted.

I can't say we discovered Big Sur by accident, but we sure didn't intend or expect the impact it had on us. About the time our boys were entering teenagerhood, we decided to take an old-fashioned family vacation spanning the US. Our version was to fly to Chicago, ride the train to LA, and drive up California Highway One to San Francisco, then to Yosemite, over the High Sierra, down to Death Valley, then on to Las Vegas and home. That whole adventure (a staple of Waddell family lore, repeated a couple of years later) provided tremendous bonding and shared experiences, but it was that drive up CA 1 that hit me and Linda between the eyes. We were entranced by the weather, the people, the stupendous scenery, the whole thing. We grew to love gazing out on those sharp edges descending to the sea and those fog banks slowly lifting in the morning, and we were always moved by being there, regardless of how many times we had been before. The place made us fall into each other all over again *because* of the memories, because of the way we took it in together.

Our first trip there, the one I described above with the whole family, was in 1980. We took the boys again in 1982 or '83 and probably visited a dozen or more times by ourselves. Sometimes we started at the northern end, flying into San Jose or Monterey. Other times, particularly in later years, we started from the southern end, flying to LAX and spending a few days at the Dallas Cowboys training camp, which was on the way from Los Angeles to Big Sur. An Amtrak train runs along the California coast, right near training camp, and once or twice we rode that train, got off in Big Sur, and made our way from there in a rental car.

Once, we got a memorable look at Big Sur from the air. Not in an airliner but in a single engine plane that took us over our favorite places: River Inn, Big Sur Post Office, Point Sur Lighthouse, Bixby Bridge. The flight was courtesy of our youngest son, Alex, who was living and working in Silicon Valley at the time and had his own plane. Part of the adventure was seeing the places we loved from another perspective, but part was being in the hands of this young man whose shoes, only yesterday, we had to tie.

In any case, we went back again and again. Whether tagged on to a business trip to the West Coast or a planned Big Sur fix, it became our place. So much so that when we planned a fiftieth anniversary gathering, it was a month in Big Sur, at a ranch overlooking that gorgeous coastline, with shifts of family and friends visiting and, we hope, sensing how much we loved each other and the place. More about that later.

I will also talk more later about Linda's passing, but one aspect of that, because it's about Big Sur, needs telling here. Linda had asked to be cremated, and I chose to leave some of her ashes in Big Sur. Her sister, Judy, agreed to go with me, so we spent a few days in Big Sur doing just that. Linda and I had a dozen or so favorite spots, and we visited each of them, leaving a little of Linda in each one: from the River Inn to Lucia to Big Sur proper, and even places outside Big Sur like the Danish town of Solvang. In a way, it was a very sad journey, and more than one tear was shed, but it made me feel close to Linda's memory and glad of the life we had had together. I couldn't have done it alone, and I'm grateful to Judy for going with me.

28

Ocean City

OCEAN CITY, MARYLAND, became a favorite destination when the boys were growing up. A friend and client of mine owned a condo right on the beachfront, with plenty of room and a balcony that looked out on the beautiful Ocean City beach and the Atlantic. We spent a week or two there for quite a few summers, swimming, sunning, and fooling around on the boardwalk. My friend spent a lot of time in another condo he owned a couple of buildings down the beach, so we would play tennis or share a meal with him and his wife on a regular basis. Our boys were young then, so after they were in bed, Linda and I shared many a glass of wine, enjoying that balcony and the view.

Linda was a good swimmer, but I could barely swim, so the time we spent *in* the ocean was spent in the surf. We really enjoyed body surfing or using a blow-up raft as a vehicle and were as happy to see big waves as a real surfer would be.

For the first forty years I knew Linda, she was determined to have the world's best suntan. Needless to say, she presented an amazing picture with her natural beauty, incredible swimsuit figure, blond hair, and deep tan. So, some of our beach time was about acquiring and maintaining that tan. In our younger years, we weren't as careful with our skin as we should have been. I particularly remember a day trip to the beach (from Richmond, I think) when we spent the whole day surfing and baking without enough, or maybe any, protection. It was overcast and windy that day, so we probably didn't feel the sun as much as usual. When we got ready to leave, we realized we had downright dangerous burns. Everywhere. Ears, the soles of our feet, everywhere. Sunburns always get worse the next day, and we ended up needing medical care at the ER back in Richmond. We paid more attention to protection after that.

Linda paid a price later in life for all that tanning: skin cancers. Her dermatologist was very insistent that she get checked frequently, so luckily, none of them got to the life-threatening stage.

But back to Ocean City. Oddly, there was a direct flight from Ocean City to Richmond in those days, so sometimes, especially when we were there for a couple of weeks, I had to make a quick trip home to attend to business. Remember, there was no email then, and even fax machines were hard to find. I always hated leaving, but it couldn't always be avoided.

Aside from spending time with my friend, we did pretty much what you would expect. The boys were around six to fourteen, so in addition to beach time, we played Putt-Putt, visited the game arcades, shopped the shops, and played tennis. All our kids have great memories of those times. Even after my friend sold that condo and the kids were grown, Linda and I still loved the place. Several times, we went for a long weekend, found a place overlooking the ocean, got a glass of wine, and relived our Ocean City memories.

2 9

Jacksonville

YOU MIGHT SAY this was an involuntary trip. In 2008, I was diagnosed with prostate cancer. After getting all the tests, I began to consider alternatives, one of which was proton beam therapy. Radiation is one of the proven treatments for this type of cancer and has about the same efficacy record as surgery and other treatments. Proton therapy is a type of radiation but has significant advantages in terms of side effects. It requires *very* expensive equipment and at the time was relatively new. It's a series of forty daily treatments, but they have to be spaced out, so the time span is more like a couple of months. I decided I wanted this treatment, but at that time, there were only eight such facilities in the US. Because of the time commitment, I would have to live in another place for two months.

By chance, there was a proton beam facility in Jacksonville, Florida, run by the University of Florida, and my law firm had a good-sized office in Jacksonville. So, Linda and I began prepping for an eight- to ten-week stay in that city. As always, Linda was by my side and on my side, and as disruptive as it was, it made me feel that we were on an adventure together. We had just gotten our second Bernese, Teddy, so our plans had to include him.

The Florida Proton Therapy Institute isn't in the most upscale area of Jacksonville, but we thought it would be convenient to live near both the institute and our Jacksonville office, so we found a townhouse in an area near downtown that had just begun to gentrify. Some people to whom we described the location thought it was a little iffy, but we were comfortable enough. I had about a twenty-minute walk to the institute and about a twenty-five-minute walk (in the opposite direction) to work. The doctors said exercise was a very good thing to fend off any fatigue the treatments might cause, so I mostly walked, although I needed to get a ride each day from my office to the institute for my treatment, so Linda usually picked me up, and we got to spend time together in the middle of the day, which was unusual.

My law practice was slowing down a little by then (I had begun to "phase out" in 2005), and that summer I spent a lot of my time revising and updating the casebook I had written for my class at UVA. Exactly when and where I worked on that project was flexible, so Linda and I got to spend more time than usual together in the evenings. One of our favorite things to do was take Teddy for a long walk around the neighborhood. Unlike in Norfolk, he had no doggie door to a backyard, so we took him out for a relief break as often as we could. We made nodding acquaintances nearby, and Teddy befriended, of all things, a cat. This cat lived a few doors away and was apparently an "outdoor cat." When Teddy walked by, she (he?) would appear out of nowhere. Teddy evidently liked her from the beginning. They would touch noses and say hello, and sometimes she would even roll over on her back and try to play. We looked for her every night.

Another thing we did involved the bridges in Jacksonville. Jacksonville is laid out on either side of the St. Johns River, so there are lots of bridges, and they are painted in a variety of colors. Three that are right downtown are red, green, and blue, respectively, and are often known by their colors (the "blue bridge," for example). They are pedestrian-friendly, so a Jacksonville-like thing to do on a nice day is to walk across one of them, stroll along the bank, and walk a different one back. Linda's hips and back weren't too bad in

2008, so we did exactly that. Several miles, I guess, all told. Although we hadn't really counted on going that far, we survived it and made some great memories sharing the views. Years later we talked about walking across those bridges, holding hands.

The final memory I will mention of Jacksonville is of a little neighborhood movie theater. Around the country, a few of these have survived the megacomplexes, and we were delighted to discover one in Jacksonville. I especially remember seeing *The Notebook* there. That movie is about young love, love later in life, and how love can transcend even death. I guess I recall that night so vividly because Linda was so touched by that story and cried over it so much, which wasn't a usual thing for her to do, that it stuck in my mind. Linda and I had been together since we were young, we were both getting old, and I had cancer, so maybe I should have seen the emotion coming. In any case, I remember that night in Jacksonville.

30

Jamaica

I NEED TO MENTION one more destination since it was such a favorite and we were there so many times. Our visits to Jamaica grew out of my friendship with a woman I'll call Amy, not her real name because she's a very private person. Amy and I met when our kids attended the same private school, and we became involved in school activities and management. We found that we liked each other a lot. We worked together on that school's affairs for decades, loved debating politics, and she really became my best friend, aside from Linda, of course.

Amy's sister owned an incredibly lovely place in a Jamaican resort. Amy borrowed it once in a while, and one cold February in 1999 (I think it was) Linda and I found ourselves in this gorgeous house in Tryall, Jamaica. It was without a doubt the most luxurious experience in a private home that I have ever had. The house itself could only be called amazing, but it was also fully staffed, so cooking, cleaning, laundry, etc., were all taken care of. The staff greeted us upon arrival, all lined up and attentive, much as important guests were greeted in *Downton Abbey*. Unlike in aristocratic England, however, this staff was treated with absolute dignity and were as friendly and companionable as one could imagine. Stays there could only be called a pampered experience, with golf, tennis, swimming, fishing, working out in the gym, or just reading and hanging out, all at hand.

The only problem was that these visits sometimes seemed to be born under a black cloud. I was basically a "deal lawyer," and during the first visit, fate dealt me deal troubles I couldn't avoid and couldn't delegate. Technology then wasn't what it is now, particularly in Jamaica, so I found myself at all hours, to my embarrassment, hovering over a fax machine, trying to get phone calls through, and not being very good company. Fortunately, Linda was Linda, and Amy and the other house guests got to know the Waddells through her.

There were many subsequent visits, three of which were also disrupted in various ways. Once, Linda couldn't come because her mom was very near death, and two other times, we had very sick dogs for whom we had to return early. Amy was as graceful about these disruptions as she was about everything else; she was all sympathy and no umbrage, although she did tease me a little about checking my dog's health before actually boarding the airplane next time.

Thanks, Amy, for those unforgettable visits.

31

San Salvador

THE LAST TRIP I want to mention was to San Salvador, but maybe not the one you're thinking. The capital of El Salvador, in Central America, is San Salvador, but the one I mean is an island in the Bahamas. A few years after I joined my law firm, one of our clients began a real estate development venture on San Salvador. The island is so named because it was the first landfall of Christopher Columbus, and he was moved to name it San Salvador (translation: Holy Savior) in thanks for making it across the Atlantic. Thus, the real estate project was known, and is known today, as Columbus Landings. I was assigned to the account and somehow wrangled an invitation to visit the project.

It wasn't easy to get there. This was 1970 or so, and although there were no commercial flights as such, our client had a way to get there (a kind of semiregular charter, as I remember) on an old DC-3. I mean an actual DC-3, where you had to walk uphill from the back to the front, chew gum when the altitude changed, and shout to be heard over the piston engines, which were a foot or two away from the cabin. Our flight was during the day, but the airstrip had no lights, so if a plane wanted to land at night, the residents of the island lined up their cars—with their lights on—on either side of the runway. Just like in the movies. We saw it a couple of times while we were there.

Anyway, we got there and found what I can only describe as an unspoiled paradise. Okay, not *completely* unspoiled. There was a motel and restaurant and a few shops, but once you got to the beach, it felt as if you were the very first human to set foot there. I remember walking down to the surf for the first time and being amazed at the powdery, stark white, utterly untouched sand. At water's edge, a little past the surf, you could see right to the sandy bottom, still white. I've never been to a place, before or since, that felt so pristine.

In addition to just hanging out on the beach, we ate fish just out of the net and were amazed at how much better it was than fish only a few hours old. We found bikes to rent, rode entirely around the perimeter of the island, and then hung out on the beach some more. Pretty close to heaven.

Making Friends with Lonesome George (1899-2012),
Galapagos Islands

Street Name Coincidence in Key West

Linda and a Friend She Named Clyde the Camel in Morocco

A Pretty Girl, Somewhere, Preparing to Board a Train

Mimicry in Ketchikan, Alaska

Staff Friends in Jamaica

PART V
Weaving: Our Connections

THIS PART IS a collection of miscellaneous things that were important to us. Some are people or events, and some are... something else. I include them here simply because they say something about us or just because I want to remember them.

3 2

Elizabeth

ONCE IN A WHILE, there is a Third that means so much to the First Two that they couldn't have been what they were without her. Elizabeth was such a person to us. Elizabeth was a cleaner/governess/friend who was with us for the years when our three boys were growing up and remained a friend until she passed away in her nineties a few years ago. Calm, stalwart, often wiser than we were, she allowed Linda a little freedom and me to maintain the breakneck pace that my nature required. Indeed, Elizabeth solved or at least ameliorated some of the domestic bumps that diverted Linda and me from each other. Looking back, she allowed us to be a little less into daily trivia and a little more into each other. Maybe only once a week, but it mattered.

Years later, Elizabeth recalled occasions when Linda left her with all three of our kids (before they were in school) so Linda could run errands or just have some time off. At least one in diapers, and at least two crying because Mommy was leaving. Elizabeth remembered this not by way of complaining but as a fond memory, with her usual good cheer and warmth.

Elizabeth (never Liz or Beth) lived more or less on the other side of the city of Richmond, and on the days she came to our house, she had to ride the bus (maybe a series of buses), making a long, long day. Always there, always cheerful, always without complaint. We got to know her family and help her a little in her declining years, and our grown children got to reunite with her. We were proud to have had her in our lives.

33

Bill's Health

THIS SECTION WILL be a lot about confessions, so get ready.

Linda and I failed to acknowledge the role of stress in our lives. My life was filled with it. Partly, this was just in the genetic nature of things. My mother used to say of my father, "He does *everything* like he's killing snakes." Which was true. My dad was driven to go the last mile, be the best, do his best, and get the best result, whatever he was doing. It wasn't that he was frenetic, or even intense. If you met him, he was reserved and polite; the word most often used to describe him was "gentleman." But he required of himself and those around him that things be done right, and sometimes that took things like time and energy and focus and determination. He was a real leader, although low-key. As a football coach, for example, he almost never raised his voice, certainly never cursed, but his players knew Coach Waddell's dedication to winning, and they would have given the last ounce and run through brick walls for him.

I inherited only the "killing snakes" part. Work, partying, long hours, demanding perfection, inventing new ways, giving 110 percent, etc. I used to tell people I might be outsmarted or overpowered, but what I would never be is outworked. Looking back, some of that intensity served me well, and some didn't, and Linda saw both results. I got to be partner of this and president or chair of that, and we enjoyed the fruits, both of my career and of other snakes I killed, but it took a toll, and from time to time I flirted with a real breakdown. Not the kind where you have to go to rehab or "the home," but the kind where light tranquilizers become a way of life, where alcohol sometimes seems a necessity, and where the people around you start trying to get you straight.

There was a year or two in college where that would have fairly described me, but that was college, after all. The time that affected me and Linda was sort of mid-career, in my thirties and early forties. I was building a reputation, clients, expertise, experience, and financial security, all mixed in with some partying. Sort of *Mad Men*. Only if there was anything left over did it go to family. Work-life balance was still largely West Coast heresy in those days. Trouble is, that isn't where my heart really was. I loved Linda and my kids, and every time I had to kill a snake, my body (not my head) charged me a stress fee. Such fees, wherever the body keeps them, eventually come due. When mine did, I ignored the warning signs and plowed ahead, which, of course, generated more fees.

My wonderful Linda took care of me through all that: the trips to the ER for something like a panic attack; covering for missed family or friend affairs; blood pressure scares; nights when I came home only in the wee hours; vacations ruined by my near-immobility; going with me for endless tests (sometimes hospitalized); and, finally, when I began to have heart issues, some real and some imagined, having the patience to help me figure out the difference. Through all this, Linda was understanding, loving, and cheerful. There's a real talent in being supportive of someone who doesn't think they need it, and Linda had that talent. Her love and touch during all those times were among the things I didn't recognize enough or appreciate enough at the time. Thank you, honey. You were the reason I got better.

3 4

Kids

LINDA MADE NO SECRET of the fact that she always wanted a daughter. Having grown up with two sisters and been a child of the fifties, when girls were thoroughly girls, she would have loved to have had a little girl to dress and teach. But, of course, she was joyful to have boys and adapted to our three, learning the ways of boys as happily and capably as everything else she did. And in the end, in a sort of indirect way, Linda's dream was realized when our youngest son produced two beautiful daughters.

Two of our sons married into families that were in some sense immigrants. Rob, our eldest, married a lovely Korean girl, actually born in Korea of Korean parents, who had lived in the US since she was a year old. She is very pretty, distinctly Korean, but her first language is pure North Carolinian, which can come as a cute surprise when you first meet her. Their wedding was a combination of a traditional American and a traditional Korean wedding. The ceremony was Christian, since her parents are Christian, but the reception included a number of Korean ceremonial customs. For example, the bride and groom, by then fully decked out in traditional Korean dress, bowed to their parents and families, and the groom carried the bride piggyback around the center table, signifying, we were told, a commitment to lifelong love and devotion. The whole event was charming and moving and brought the two families closer.

The other wedding with "foreign" elements was that of our youngest son, Alex, who married a girl, also very pretty, whose father was born in India. His work took him all over the world, but he and his family maintained very close ties with his Indian relatives and heritage. As with Rob, the ceremony was traditional Christian, but Indian customs were woven into other parts of the wedding weekend. Most memorable was the Sangeet, which is an Indian tradition that roughly corresponds to a rehearsal dinner. Most of the guests, even those not of Indian heritage, dressed in traditional Indian garb (I was in a dhoti, I think), took part in traditional Indian things like a stick dance, and encountered some Indian dishes they had perhaps not had before.

Linda was, as usual, beautiful and charming at both weddings. I used a picture taken of her at Alex's wedding in her obituary and as the signature photo at her memorial service. We counted ourselves lucky to be a part of these international celebrations.

The wedding of our middle son, Keith, was lovely also. He was the first of our sons to marry. The ceremony itself, and the reception, which was in a private club atop a tall building, were wonderful. That marriage led to two cherished grandsons, but unfortunately didn't last, but that's another story, for another day.

The challenges, happiness, and travails of raising three boys are beyond the scope of our love story, but our boys, all of whom are successful, although in very different ways, remain our proudest accomplishment and pleasure. We were all by her side when she died.

3 5

Homes

I'VE ALREADY DESCRIBED our home in Charlottesville. Moving from there to Richmond, we rented a house (larger than we needed) in kind of a semirural location in southwest Richmond for the first year. The house sat back from the road about 150 yards, there were lots of trees around, it was quiet, and we enjoyed a kind of cabin-in-the-woods thing for those months. I was excited about my new job, and we had two incomes for the first time. Having only one car, and with Linda working at an office downtown not far from mine, we commuted together. Best of all, Linda was pregnant. Life was good.

Unfortunately, all this became a problem when a surprise late-winter snowstorm started one afternoon, continued into the evening, and eventually ended up accumulating more than a foot. We had just bought a Ford Mustang, not exactly built for deep snow, and by the time I picked Linda up, driving had become pretty dicey. Southern cities, after all, aren't usually that good at dealing with a foot of snow. As we drove out of Richmond, city streets became more country roads, things got even more dicey, and when we turned into our long dirt driveway, I began to get really scared. It was dark by then, and there weren't even tracks to guide us. The Mustang got irrevocably stuck (it stayed there for several days), and as far as I could see, our only choices (remember it was long before cell phones) were to stay in the car or try to slog toward our house.

No boots, no big coats, and one of us pregnant.

For some reason, one of the first survival rules I thought of was that you have to keep moving or you will freeze to death. We probably wouldn't have (surely, someone would have come along at some point), but for some reason this rule was foremost in my mind, and I was determined to get Linda into the house. The snow was deep enough that we had to work at getting the car doors open, but we did. We started marching toward the house, snow in our eyes and in our shoes, with little light to show the way. I dragged Linda along even though she desperately wanted to rest. I shouted that we had to keep moving, and she shouted back, "I CAN'T! I'M PREGNANT, YOU KNOW!" But we made it, none the worse for wear, built a fire, and spent a couple of days playing board games and watching daytime TV. Not so bad.

Our next home was on a city street much nearer downtown: a little white house that was in a nice neighborhood and for which we paid, in 1966, the princely sum of $12,000. Three tiny bedrooms, no utility room, so the washing machine (no dryer) was in a closet. I actually added a room on the back of that house so we could have a washer and dryer, using an old US Army manual that showed how to build WWII barracks, wiring, plumbing, and all.

All our three sons lived in that house, although by the time Alex (our third) came along in 1970, we were bulging at the seams, so we soon moved to what became our long-term Richmond house on Fernleigh Drive. It was in a very nice neighborhood, one that was not in vogue at that time, so we got a lot of footage for the money: nearly 4,000 square feet, including a finished basement (actually terrace-level) apartment that we used as an office/library and entertainment space.

The love and attention Linda gave that house was extraordinary. I was buried in my career by then, so decorating all that space fell to her, and she excelled at it. I helped when asked, but from color schemes to artwork to furnishings, that house was her baby. During those first few years on Fernleigh, her family and her house were her life; she was devoted to them, and she was *really* good at them. And we found lifelong friends in that time. The couples who lived directly across the street and right next door are friends to this day.

In 1990 or so, my law firm acquired a large firm in Northern Virginia, and I took a post as liaison between the "home office" in Richmond and the new one in Tysons Corner (Fairfax). It required me to be there several days a week, so I took an apartment (unfurnished) in a development within walking distance of my Tysons office. Our place in Wintergreen (more about this special skiing location later) was on the market, so the furniture at Wintergreen became the furniture at Tysons Corner. One of the nicest things Linda ever did for me was arrange that move. I was covered up with the job I had taken on, constantly back and forth, meeting people, keeping my own practice going while helping merge the two firms administratively and politically, and I had no time for anything else. So when I walked into this apartment a day or two after I signed up for it, and found it fully cleaned, furnished, and set up with familiar things, down to the coffee cups, I was stunned. Linda had arranged and supervised *everything*, as a surprise. It was a good one.

I guess you could say our move from Richmond to Norfolk was bittersweet. I had a large client in the Norfolk area, the managing partner in our Norfolk office was retiring, and my firm was putting some heat on me—offering some real incentives—to take it over, so there were some significant items on the pro side of the ledger. On the other side, though, were our roots in Richmond: other clients, familiar places, and, most important, friends, particularly Linda's friends. She made really close friends throughout her life—that's just how she was. And she kept them forever. So when I broached the subject of moving to Norfolk, her first thought was of losing close friendships. Closest of all was Marilyn, from across the street, who was truly her dearest and best friend. Moving was the right thing for both of us, and in the end, it worked out wonderfully well, but at its heart, it was a career move for me and a hard transition for Linda, and I loved her so much for doing it.

We lived in a rented townhouse in Downtown Norfolk for a year, getting our feet on the ground and deciding where we wanted to settle. We had always been suburban dwellers but found city life much to our liking and decided to buy a freestanding house in the same area as the townhouse, just a couple of blocks away. I loved the short commute and walked to work in nice weather. We had great neighbors and found ways to help our doggies adapt. As always, Linda took great pleasure in, and was very good at, renovating and decorating our new digs. I still live in that house.

3 6

Second Homes

I WANT TO MENTION these because they meant so much to us and were the source of so much enjoyment—of the homes and of each other. There were two, as different as could be. The first was at Wintergreen, a mountain ski resort about two or three hours west of Richmond. Although neither of us skied, we kind of fell in love with the place anyway. We had rented a place there a couple of times, and when they began building some new condos, we jumped in. It wasn't very big, just one bedroom, one bath, and a sleeping loft. That was about the time the kids were leaving home, so we weren't often there all at one time. In any event, we squeezed ourselves in and spent a lot of happy times there. Later, either because they had left the nest or just didn't want to go, the kids weren't there so much, so it was just me and Linda, cozied up by the fire when it was cold or enjoying our little balcony in warmer weather. Eventually, I guess it ran its course, and we sold it in the early nineties.

The second second home was at the beach. We had close friends with whom we had rented houses at the beach for a decade or more, and we had toyed with the idea of building our own place. We never did much about it, though, until I agreed to take over my law firm's Norfolk office in 1992. Norfolk is about forty-five minutes from the section of Virginia Beach we had gone to most, Sandbridge. Sandbridge, a spit of land lying right between the Atlantic Ocean and Back Bay, is about four miles long and maybe 500 yards wide. Its beachfront has a checkered past, in that its sand has come and gone, as have some beachfront houses. As this is being written, its beach is beautiful and stable, and a sand replenishment program is intended to keep it that way.

We bought property there when Sandbridge's future was uncertain. For Linda, this was the dream of a lifetime and helped ease the disruption of uprooting from Richmond. She *loved* the beach and everything about it. A true second home *on* the beach wasn't something we could afford easily, and we were uneasy about the erosion issue, so we decided on a kind of compromise. We bought a lot four rows back from the beachfront and built a house in a configuration we could easily rent. At the time, there weren't any houses between us and the actual beachfront, so we had an excellent view. Our plan worked wonderfully well. We rented it during the summer high season and enjoyed it the rest of the year ourselves. Linda and I were never closer than we were during that planning, looking, building, and settling in/renting process. Because we had usually been with friends or family or both when we were at the beach, it was a new treat for us when we could just walk or swim or sun ourselves *by* ourselves. It was fun, exciting, relatively trouble-free, and a good investment.

When the house turned twenty years old, though, it came time to make some decisions, and two basic things had changed between 1993 and 2015: First, as the erosion risk had come under control, several houses had been built between us and the beachfront, greatly interfering with our view. Second, Linda was beginning to have some significant mobility issues. She was using a cane after post-op from her back surgery.

These two things, *and* the fact that you could now safely build living space on the ground floor, combined to move us toward "reorienting" our beach house from beach-facing to bay-facing. We finished off the ground floor, spruced up the backyard, put in a pool, built a guesthouse adjacent to the pool, renovated the interior, and, most importantly, installed an elevator. A lot of this spanned the time she was in Baltimore for her back surgery, so she got to see part of it (the pool and elevator, for example) for the first time after it was completed. She kissed me, teared up, and just said Thank You.

37

Walking

MUNDANE A TOPIC as this may be, walking played a role for Linda and me. More at some points than others, but always a role. I've never really reflected on it much until right now. From the time we met until we moved to Norfolk, we never really had much occasion to walk together. Linda was a fairly serious exercise walker, and I was a pretend runner, but with a few exceptions, we did those separately. Of course, we would take the kids for walks when they were small, and there were a few times when the spirit moved us to a hike in the woods (at Wintergreen, for example, where the Appalachian Trail ran near our condo), but for the most part, it wasn't one of our things. When we moved to Norfolk, though, it became part of our relationship.

To some extent, this was prompted by having to walk our faithful golden, Barney. Although there were times when Barney escaped and roamed around Norfolk by himself, we were generally afraid to let him out in the urban area where we lived, so two or three walks with him became a daily routine. Often, we would go together, particularly in the evening, and we gradually realized how much we were enjoying these walks, discovering the neighborhood and just being together. Our neighborhood is a lovely inner-city oasis, densely populated but with meticulously kept dwellings and lots of green spaces. We covered all these streets, met lots of people, found Barney's favorite places, and debated whether Street A was prettier than Street B.

Then we began walking as a way of getting around: the grocery store, drugstore, Blockbuster, the ice-cream place. Some were quite nearby, but soon we found ourselves walking to places we would not have thought of walking to before. One of our favorites was to our small movie theater, one of those wonderful places out of the forties and fifties that sometimes showed first-run movies but sometimes "art films" or old classics. It was about a twenty-minute walk along quiet tree-lined streets, and we sometimes went early and had dinner at a street café, but usually just walked, held hands, and, on the way back, talked about the movie we saw.

It was about a thirty-minute walk from our house to my office building. For many years, I walked to work. Not every day, because some days I needed a car, but otherwise I walked rain or snow, hot or cold. Sometimes Linda would say, "Are you *really* going to walk today?" and I would almost always say yes. I kind of took pride in it.

I don't go to my office every day now, and when I *do* go, I don't walk. I've substituted a long walk with Bodie, about the same distance, in late afternoon. Which reminds me, Linda didn't give up walking with her beloved dogs until she got really sick. The fact that she was a little unstable on her feet, and routinely used a cane, never held her back. Every time she went for one of these walks, I worried about her getting pulled too hard and taking a fall, but every time, she came back and said everything had gone fine.

But aside from all these purposeful trips, I guess the best walks were still the ones where we weren't going anywhere in particular, just touching and falling into a rhythm and seeing if there was anything new to see.

3 8

Not Monkey Business

SOME OF YOU will remember that a (married) candidate for president, one Gary Hart, was obliged to drop out of the race when a somewhat suggestive photo with a lady, not his wife, suddenly appeared in the national press. The photo itself wouldn't have been so bad, probably, as it wasn't *that* suggestive, and other politicians have survived worse. The problem was that Hart was wearing a T-shirt that said *Monkey Business*. Turns out this was the name of a luxury yacht on which Hart and the young lady had recently been spotted on the way to Bimini. No politician (except maybe Bill Clinton) could have survived that. This all happened in the early 1970s.

As it happens, the law firm for which I worked had a (married) partner who was rather well-known, one might even say famous, as a ladies' man. Tall, handsome guy, with—you guessed it—a nice yacht that he kept in a nearby coastal area. I'm not going to mention his name, although his infidelities became quite public later, albeit on a more local scale than Mr. Hart's. Let's call him Jim. It was more or less traditional for Jim to invite new associates at the firm to spend a long weekend on his boat. To be fair, it was quite welcoming and friendly for him to do that, and new kids on the block, like me, looked forward to it. There was fishing and cruising and sunning and imbibing, and everyone enjoyed it.

Now, in those days, most new associates were guys, so the outing was also a male bonding experience, kind of a rite of passage. Some of us were married, and some of us were not, and Jim's reputation was regarded differently, of course, by the single guys and the married guys (and their wives). The former traded stories and rumors with great anticipation, while the latter told their wives (and may have believed) that it was all made up. All things considered, it is probably fair to say there was something between a whiff and a miasma of monkey business surrounding these trips.

I was invited to this weekend a few months after I joined the firm. We arrived for the adventure late on a Friday, after dinner (this was the custom, so as to allow us to leave after work), were shown where to stow our gear and what the safety rules of the vessel were, and hit the bunks early, anticipating reveille at dawn. As promised, it was a great day on the water, and by midafternoon, we were ready for a cleanup and nap.

Dinner was at the resort where Jim kept the boat, complete with live music and merrymakers from the resort and surrounding area. I am going to omit the details of that evening; suffice it to say that Jim lived up to his reputation as a charmer of the fairer sex, and it was a late night. Next morning, we dragged ourselves out of our berths, had some coffee and what passed for breakfast, and prepared to drag ourselves home.

Now I'll reveal why I'm sharing this story. We had had some incidental meals on the boat—lunch and a couple of breakfasts—and had accumulated some dirty dishes. Everyone had a job on this crew, and part of my assignment was to wash these dishes and police up the trash. The galley on the boat was small, so we were told to take some soap and do them on a nearby dock area that had running water. You know, one of those dock areas with a walkway made of wooden slats and a garden hose nearby. Easy.

The other thing you need to know is that my wedding ring was too big. Always had been. I fiddled with it constantly and had intended to get it resized for years, but I never got around to it.

You can see it coming. Soapy hands. A loose wedding ring. Half a hangover. Sure enough, the ring slipped off and fell between the slats and into the water below.

The guy who was with me on this assignment instantly recognized the deeply dangerous situation I was in. No human being who knew Jim's reputation would believe I had not taken the ring off voluntarily. My potential witnesses were compromised since they were themselves involved in this suspect venture. I immediately began calculating just how much trust I had accumulated in my marriage bank.

Fortunately, my companion in the dishwashing assignment, a guy named Paul, was more resourceful than I. He was as horrified as I was but had the presence of mind to suggest that all was not lost, that perhaps we could scrape the sediment under the dock and find the ring, or maybe we could use a metal detector. I more or less ridiculed this idea, but he ran off to find equipment. He came back with a net, the kind you use to land a fish, with a long handle. The water was shallow right under the walkway, so I was able to lean over the side and have the net reach the sandy bottom. One scrape. Two. I don't know how many it took, but eventually, to my astonishment and relief, we brought up the net, and there among the sand and shells was my wedding ring. I told Paul he was an absolute hero. He didn't think it was as unlikely a recovery as I did.

I told Linda this story when I got home. As I was describing the dishwashing and the slipperiness and how my ring had come off, she actually said, "Oh, sure," as if Monkey Business had been going on for sure. Then she saw that the ring was in fact back on my hand, which made my story a bit more plausible. Taken together, all this proved that my fears of what might have happened had I not recovered the ring had been well-founded. Our relationship would surely have survived, but over the years, Linda might have had a niggling little suspicion that perhaps I had lost my ring (under iffy circumstances) and had to make up a cover story. No one needs that.

39

Tennis

AS I'VE NOTED, sometimes Linda lost interest and moved on when she got far enough into something that was no longer a complete challenge. This didn't happen with the game of tennis. I can't remember the first time Linda and I played; it was probably in high school. But our serious tennis-playing times were after we moved to Richmond in 1965. Now, if you're old enough, you remember that the golden age of tennis *playing* (not necessarily the height of the professional sport) in the US was in the seventies and early eighties, so we fit right in. Tennis was wildly popular. *Everyone* was playing; courts (outdoor and indoor, hard and clay) were everywhere, and tennis shops were on every corner. We joined a neighborhood tennis facility, and later a country club, and tennis became an important part of our lives. We met many of our friends from playing tennis and spent a lot of time playing, watching, or attending social events built around tennis. We often took our racquets when we travelled, and many of the conventions and meetings we went to included a tournament. Sometimes I would sneak out of work early just to play with her.

I was never very good, although I played on a club "fun" team and could usually beat Linda in singles. She was a much better women's player than I was a men's, with a serve that was very troublesome even for good players, and people were surprised that I could win when she and I played singles. There was some suspicion that she was letting me win, but she denied it. She played on a legitimate club team, got asked to play in lots of member-guest tournaments, and won lots of trophies, cups, and plaques. I still have those, and I treasure them.

We really enjoyed playing each other. We were very competitive in the sense that each of us wanted to win, but there was never a trace of anger or even irritation when we played. It was sharing something we both liked. And it was the same when we played mixed doubles, which we did a lot. Even when one of us made a mistake, even a stupid one, we just played on and had fun. I have great memories of those years.

Alas, Linda tore her ACL in the eighties. It was repaired, and she went back to playing, but it was never quite the same for her. A decade or so after that, her back and hip troubles began, which brought her playing days to a close. I played a little after that, but not much; my interest in tennis was too closely tied up with hers. The last time I had a racquet in my hand was on one of the Jamaica trips, maybe five years ago. Some of the house guests and I just hit a few balls around for fun. Linda went down to the courts with us, and I remember cajoling her into picking up a racquet, going out on the court, cane and all, and hitting a few. It was probably not a very safe thing for her to do, but she thought it was fun. I guess I just wanted to remember our tennis days one more time.

4 0

... And Automobiles

LIKE PLANES, TRAINS, AND BOATS, these played a role in our respective lives and in our love story. The first car I can remember Linda driving was a little Austin-Healey, white with a black convertible top. She was extremely proud of that car, and indeed it was pretty exotic for the mid-century Midwest, especially when being driven by this gorgeous girl with flowing blond hair. I got to ride in it a few times, and I actually took it home once.

But it was soon put in the shade by a 1960 Thunderbird convertible, mint green and fully loaded. The Ford Thunderbird, along with the Chevy Corvette, had taken the (already-car-crazy) country by storm in the mid-fifties. Ford was a pioneer in making power retracting hardtops, and Linda's T-bird model (along with the Ford Skyliner) was among the first production examples. Lots of people had never seen a hard convertible top that went down—and was hidden—at the touch of a button. Count me among those people, so I was truly impressed.

Exuberant doesn't begin to describe her attitude about that car. She looked great in it (I think she chose the color to match her eyes) and was moderately famous for having it. Trouble is, she owed a lot of money on it. Maybe not more than she could have managed in her present circumstances (single with a good job), but far more than a couple of starving students could handle. I looked at the giant monthly payment and began hinting that it would have to be sold. Linda, needless to say, was brokenhearted at this prospect. We tried every angle we could think of to avoid her having to part with it, but in the end, we had to let it go in favor of a cheaper alternative. Linda eventually accepted this as inevitable, but deep down I think it was still painful, and I felt bad for her. Over the years, she gave me a lot of ribbing about the fact that I made her sell her T-bird, always good-naturedly, but maybe with some remembered sadness.

Perhaps that had something to do with a later purchase. After we went through the usual succession of practical station wagons, etc., and the kids were mostly grown, I encouraged her to get something she could really enjoy. This turned out to be a red Ford Mustang convertible with a big V8 engine. We ordered it through a dealer in Northern Virginia because it saved a few bucks, and Linda took a bus or train or something up there and picked it up. A powerful car it was, but somehow elegant.

I was working partly in Northern Virginia at the time but had a meeting back in Richmond on the day she picked it up. I was riding down I-95 with one of my partners, talking about our meeting, when I glanced over into the next lane, and what did I see but a red Mustang convertible, doing a good seventy-five mph, the top down, with a beautiful blond—yes, my Linda—behind the wheel. I waved desperately to get her attention, and we both pulled over for an admiring chat. I don't know if she loved that car as much as the T-bird, but I hope so. Sadly, it was totaled after less than a year by one of our sons, but we replaced it almost exactly with the next year's model.

I was probably still trying to shed my T-bird guilt a few years later when Linda's car became a bright red (naturally) BMW M Roadster convertible. The M was a true sports car, as fast as a muscle car but nimbler. She loved it but found it a little impractical for picking up anything larger than a breadbox, so we moved on. We sold it to a lady who came to pick it up early one morning. She left a cashier's check, which I left lying on my briefcase so I could deposit it when I went to work. Alas, when we weren't paying attention, whichever Berner we had at the time tore up and partly consumed the check, as he often did with mail. Linda and I had to go to the local bank branch to plead our case, based on the explanation that "the dog ate our check." Fortunately, after a few phone calls, it worked out.

41

The Jaguar

TALKING ABOUT CARS may seem odd in a memoir-meets-love-story, but, like most Americans who grew up in the fifties, we had an abiding interest in cars.

The story of another important car actually begins with a train. In the summer of 1977, we arranged a trip that included a visit to Kentucky with friends and family, followed by a train trip to New England, and then to Maine and Nova Scotia. The train that was to take us to New England, however, didn't stop in the Kentucky area where we were. We had to catch it in Richmond, Indiana, which was a good couple of hours away, and it came through Richmond in the very late evening. Nonetheless, we were determined to experience this train route, one we had not been on before, so we trooped up to Richmond, turned in our rental car, and made our way to the train depot. Richmond, Indiana, was a "whistle-stop," meaning that the train stopped there *only* if there were passengers getting on or off, so the depot wasn't really a depot at all. It was just an abandoned little building, completely unmanned. There were no other passengers, and it was dark, so the whole scene was a little spooky. There were signs indicating where one should wait, so there we were. We waited, and waited, and waited. No cell phones, of course, not even an emergency phone around the station, so we waited.

When the train was an hour or so overdue, we began thinking

about alternatives. There was some sort of bar or tavern across the road, but I was afraid that if I went over to try to call Amtrak, the damn train would come. So we waited.

Around about midnight, we were all (especially the kids) very tired and decided we had to chance going over to the bar. Fortunately, they had a pay phone, from which I called Amtrak and found out, confirming my worst fears, that there would be no train. It had wrecked somewhere to the west of us, and there would be no replacement. There was exactly one train a day through Richmond, so the next one would be late evening the next day. We had no car, and no place to get a car, but managed to get a taxi to a motel.

Richmond, Indiana, is somewhere between a small town and a very small city, so finding a way to kill time while waiting for a night train is not easy. But fate was smiling on us, and we found two interesting things to do. The first was *Star Wars*. The movie had just come out, and there was a movie theater in Richmond, so that was easy. I don't remember exactly why I didn't want to go, but Linda took the boys and enjoyed it enormously.

While they were at the movie, I did the second interesting thing, which was to scan the classified ads in the local paper. In 1977 I was driving a Triumph TR-6. I had rebuilt it almost from stem to stern and was very proud of it but ready to move on to something else, so I had been watching the classifieds (the medium of choice in those days for trading cars) both for selling and buying information. What should appear in that day's classified ads in the Richmond, Indiana, paper but a 1970 British Racing Green Jaguar XKE, one of the cars of my dreams. The Jaguar XKE was and is considered among the most beautiful cars ever built. Its mechanical quality is another story, but it is truly a pretty car. This one had 14,000 miles on it and was in near-perfect condition, according to the ad, so I had to see it.

I was not disappointed. It appeared to be as represented, and I was in love. Price was something else, however, and I was unwilling to pay what the guy wanted, so we resumed our vacation. But I didn't forget. When we returned to *our* Richmond, I worried and fidgeted and researched other cars, and finally, Linda told me that if I wanted the car, I should make an offer on it or shut up. I made an offer, then another offer, and finally made a deal.

Now the question was how to get the thing from Richmond to Richmond. Having just come back from vacation, I was really jammed up from a work standpoint, so I looked into hiring a driver, having it trucked, etc., but nothing seemed to fit. Which is where my lovely Linda becomes the focus of this little story. She said the solution was very simple: She would fly out to Indiana and drive the car home. Naturally, I was horrified by the idea, but she insisted it was something she *wanted* to do and was excited about. She gave me all the reasons it made sense and may have even shamed me a little for being sexist. Finally, I agreed, and the next morning I took her to the airport.

It took less than twenty-four hours to regret the decision. Linda called me that night from someplace in Pennsylvania, saying she had left the car under an underpass on an interstate after it had simply quit. Not "developed a problem," not "started giving her trouble"— Quit. Turned out the fuel pump, famously unreliable on that car, had given out. Remember, again, how different situations like this were before we all had cell phones. She had had to flag down a state trooper, have the poor XKE towed to the closest appropriate repair facility (turned out to be in Baltimore), and somehow find her way to a motel. At least she was safe.

Linda related all this to me calmly, not in a state of panic. Not even very excitedly. I could tell she had been through a trying experience, but she was focused mostly on what was to be done. We arranged to meet the next morning. I would love to say there was no further incident, but when we visited the facility, we found that someone had tried to break into it during the night, causing some noticeable, although minor, damage. We decided to have that out with the garage later, so we arranged fuel pump repairs and drove the car home. Linda had so many wonderful layers; this showed one of the best of them.

I kept that car for several years, driving it occasionally in a rally or for fun, and sold it for a good bit more than I paid. The guy who bought it sent a car transport van and had it trucked home. I guess he was smarter than I was, but he didn't have as much fun.

4 2

Friends

IT'S HARD TO DESCRIBE the depth and significance of Linda's friendships. There were a *lot* of them. Linda was so easy to be with, so likable, that people often thought of her (and she of them) as a friend in a very short time. But there were a half dozen or so that were truly close to her. I won't try to name them, for fear of leaving someone out. I'll just call them *the friends*. Some were family, some were neighbors, and some were from tennis. These were long-term relationships, all the more remarkable since the friend didn't always live nearby, some scattered around the country.

I think it's hard for guys, particularly old guys, to understand the sisterships that sometimes develop among women. Linda's were enduring, entirely without friction (as far as I could tell), and among the most important things in her life. In early years, and even later, physical activity was a big component: tennis, exercise walks, aerobics, yoga, etc. Events were important: country music concerts, opera, and watching one of her friends play the cello. Always and often shopping. Sharing grief over kids or friends or pets.

But the most memorable times were the trips, specifically two to Europe, that lived vividly and deeply in their memories. Whenever they got together, they recounted, laughed about, and savored these trips again and again. Even when she was just with me, she enjoyed talking about the trips, and I enjoyed listening. She came alive and wanted me to enjoy the memories with her, often saying she wanted to take me to some of the places they had gone.

In a way, these trips were the focus of the last time they were all together. I say all, although by that time a couple had passed away. For years, Linda had had a "girls weekend" at our beach house. The friends would gather for good food, wine, telling of tales, and maybe some time on the beach. This was a tradition that went on for a couple of decades. They would always invite me to visit, and I may have once or twice, but the virtually exclusive mission of these weekends was bonding and reminiscing.

This tradition was interrupted, along with most everything else, by the pandemic, so there was no girls weekend in 2020. Linda was diagnosed with cancer in October of that year and rapidly became more and more ill, but in early 2021, she began talking about having such a weekend in the spring. As I look back on it, she may have seen her time coming to an end more clearly than I did, or at least more clearly than I wanted to acknowledge. In any case, we began to arrange for a gathering at the beach.

By the time it came together, Linda was *very* sick. She was weak, often not very hungry, confined to a wheelchair except for trips to the bathroom, and required heavy oxygen constantly. We had a wonderful caretaker who helped me get her to the beach house, get all the equipment in place, and settle her in. But as hard as the circumstances were, Linda's weekend was beyond joyous. We had brought all the photo albums from the European trips, and they all (including Linda) laughed and hooted over their recollections of large, small, and downright silly things: getting lost and dancing with Italian men, eating, drinking, seeing sights, and simply enjoying each other.

Every one of us knew that this was Goodbye. It hadn't been arranged that way, and it wasn't said out loud, but everyone knew, and everyone said it to Linda in various ways. It wasn't Linda's way to be tearful or maudlin, but she knew, and somewhere inside herself, she placed an incredible value on the chance to see her dearest friends one more time. It was especially good to see this happening in the setting that had seen so much pleasure and love among these friends over the years.

43

The Dallas Cowboys

I'M A DALLAS COWBOYS FAN, complete with season tickets, hats, etc. People ask how I got that way, not having any connection to Dallas, and I'm never sure of the answer. Partly, it's because my son, Alex, has always (long before I was) been a fan. Another part is because I fell into a nest of Washington Redskins followers when we moved to Virginia, didn't really like the Skins, and decided to identify with their greatest rival, the Cowboys. Besides that, they have cute cheerleaders.

Linda, on the other hand, stuck with the Redskins until about 2005, at which time she formally announced that she was switching to the Cowboys. Alex and I were delighted, as was Linda's sister, Judy, who had lived in Texas for a while.

When the Cowboys' new stadium opened in 2008, I mused with Alex about the possibility of buying season tickets. He was up for it, but when we started looking into it, we were quickly educated in the matter of "seat options," a financing tool for modern stadiums. Buying season tickets at a new facility typically requires one to fork over a lump sum that gives the buyer an *option* to buy a ticket, not the ticket itself. That comes later. The price of the option is hefty, well into five figures per seat for the location we were looking at.[8] But in the end, we (some would say recklessly) bought not two but *four* seats

---

8   For the best seats in the house, the per-seat cost is well into six figures.

in the so-called loge, on the very front row, about the forty-five-yard line, looking directly at the famous 160-foot-long jumbotron.

I have never made a better decision. They are terrific seats, we didn't quite have to take bankruptcy, and it's a wonderful place to take friends and family. Alex and I and our wives went to the very first game in the new stadium, found some delightful Mexican fans to tailgate with, and saw the midfield star uncovered, a big deal to longtime fans. This wonderful and memorable occasion was marred only slightly by the fact that the Cowboys lost at the last minute.

Linda and I went to a few games a year, sometimes inviting friends, sometimes going with Alex. We found the Sanford House, an elegant B&B right near the stadium, and soon had favorite restaurants, etc. One of our favorite Saturday hangouts was at the old Stockyards in Fort Worth, where everyone from truckers to investment bankers put on boots and a cowboy hat. I have a great picture of Linda riding a steer in front of one of the restaurants.

At the games, you would have thought Linda and I were honeymooners, laughing and celebrating and smooching after touchdowns. She loved and accumulated lots of Cowboys clothing and other gear, and when we were in Dallas, we always stopped at the Walmart across from the stadium to buy more. When we had guests, they probably thought this was a strange stop, but the store had a huge display, not only of Cowboys gear but of the visiting team as well. Apparel, yes, but in addition, everything from rolls of Cowboys paper towels to Cowboys lampshades and guitar picks. I still take guests there, and it's always mobbed on game day.

At some point, we decided to combine our shared love of the Cowboys with our shared love of Big Sur. For years, the Cowboys have held their summer training camp at the Residence Inn in Oxnard, California. Oxnard is a city of 200,000 or so about two hours north of LAX, right on the coast near Ventura. The weather is classic Central California coast: cool at night, seventies during the day, and very little rain in the summer. Despite not knowing anything about the camp or the facility, we decided to tack it on to a Big Sur trip.

It turned out to be a huge success. The Residence Inn is a sprawling motel right in Oxnard. If it didn't have signage, you would think it was a mid-price apartment development, with a large number of two-story buildings, each containing eight or ten units. During camp, the bulk of it is fenced off and becomes the training and living quarters for the team. A few units, maybe forty or so, are reserved for press, etc., and until very recently, there were a few units available to the general public if you were willing to pay enough and be persistent enough. Most years, we managed to score a second-floor unit overlooking the fenced-off area, which allowed us to spy on players, coaches, etc., as they came and went. The front desk was still open, and occasionally, a player you recognized would be seen, but there were lots of signs warning against asking for autographs. About half the actual practices were open to the public, and if you were staying at the hotel, you got a pass to watch from a sort of VIP area instead of the stands with the general public. With these passes, we actually met and got to talk to several players and coaches.

Oxnard is definitely California suburbia, although still having a lot of farming mixed in. We got to know where the good restaurants and other destinations were in Oxnard and the surrounding area. We always spent a day down in Malibu or Topanga Canyon (Charlie Manson country) or Santa Barbara or somewhere else nearby. After camp, we headed up to Big Sur, stopping off (in later years) in the charming Danish-inspired town of Solvang.

Maybe training camp doesn't sound very romantic, but it was. We never enjoyed life or each other more than when we were on the California coast, wherever we were—which leads me to our fiftieth wedding anniversary expedition.

44

The Fiftieth

LINDA AND I were married in 1962, so as 2012 approached, we began to think about how to celebrate the extraordinary fifty years we had just spent together. We thought about all the ways to throw a big party and all the trips and cruises we could take but decided we wanted to do something that we really enjoyed and invite the people closest to us to share the experience. We settled on—you guessed it—a long stay in Big Sur. Our anniversary was in August, and that's the ideal month in Big Sur, so we started planning.

The first thing we needed was a venue. We wanted to be right in Big Sur, not just near it or with access to it but right in the magic itself: the coolness and mist in the morning; the quiet at night; the incredible views of the mountains on one side and the Pacific on the other and the rough beaches where they met; the sense of removal (or at least insulation) from the modern world; and the music, which was strings or Peruvian pipes or George Winston at an acoustic piano. And we wanted to enjoy the people who lived there and painted or wove or ranched or ran shops for people like us. Many were vaguely reminiscent of people you knew or knew of from the 1960s or before: kind, gentle, intelligent, not much caring about whether they were up with the times or obeying all the rules, knowing what their values are and dedicated more to enjoying life than getting rich. We wanted the Big Sur Experience.

Hotels and motels are pretty sparse in Big Sur, and even the choices we had didn't really meet our needs, so we decided to try to rent a big house. We actually made a trip out there to look at possibilities and finally found exactly what we needed. Not a luxurious place but a big one, with the many bedrooms we needed and a view over the Big Sur coastline to die for. We booked it for a month.

We carefully scheduled family and friends on a rotating basis and sent invitations. To our delight and surprise, almost everyone said they would come, despite the fact that it required travel across the entire US. About forty people visited for some part of our celebration.

The logistics were elaborate. We didn't want to be cooking all the time, so we laid in some of the food we would need but found a lady nearby who would bring us dinner each evening. Turned out, she was really good. Sometimes she would bring an enormous fish. Other nights she made lamb or chicken or something else, all with wonderful sides and rich desserts. So she fed us dinner like kings, and the rest of the time, we fixed breakfast or sandwiches or went out to eat. It worked out just as we had hoped.

Days were spent just enjoying the ambiance, touring the Big Sur area, reading, playing games, etc. There was no TV, thank goodness, so even when the guests included kids, they had to find some in-house or local entertainment. Nights were truly magic. The house sat on a bluff overlooking the Pacific Ocean and down the coast. Along that part of the California coast, the mountains (modest, as mountains go, but still mountains) are golden in August and dive right into the water, creating rugged beaches or rocky outcroppings, with beautiful surf and sea vegetation. We spent a lot of time just absorbing that scene during the day, but it was at night that it was truly mesmerizing. Sunsets were spectacular, and everyone, wine in hand, tried to get a photo that would remind them of their experience. After dark, we found that if we turned out the lights in the house, there was virtually no light pollution at all, and since there were never clouds, the sky presented a display of stars like few of us had ever seen. The difference between a typical night in an urban area and a night unsullied by any light pollution at all is unbelievable. We could see the Milky Way very vividly, and with the help of an iPad and the right software, we could pick out planets, stars, and constellations we had only heard of and never really seen. Usually, we stayed up late and slept late.

There was a little incident one day that some of us (although not all) sort of appreciated, and that became a permanent part of our fiftieth memories. On the coast to the south of us, there was enough of a little sand beach to accommodate sunbathing and swimming and enough of a sand track to allow access, but not enough visibility (except from our house) to require a lot of modesty. Around midday one weekend, one of us noticed that there were actually people there, and this was enough of an unusual occurrence that soon there were binoculars trained on the area. It was far enough away that you couldn't really see detail with the naked eye, but with binoculars, you could see that the eye was not the only thing that was naked. Much frivolity ensued, which was thought more appropriate by some than others. In any case, it wasn't too long before the sunbathers left, it being noted that they didn't actually get dressed before leaving. Some hoped there would be similar incidents in the future, but there weren't.

One of the house's features was that it was located within a big private ranch, so you had to go a couple of miles to get from the road to the house itself. It was an actual working ranch, so there was lots of activity on the way, and the owners (our landlords) had asked that we not drive in and out too much because it disturbed the animals. This led to one of our most momentous decisions. Because I didn't want us or our guests to be stuck at the house, I decided to buy a couple of electric bicycles we could use to go down to the little village of Big Sur, where there was a restaurant, a store, a post office, and some shops. When Linda and I first arrived, we had no small amount of luggage, food, and other supplies, so we had no room for the bikes I had planned to pick up from a dealer in Monterrey.

After we unloaded, I went back to Monterrey, picked up the bikes, and brought them back to the house, where I excitedly mounted one to show Linda how cool they were, how useful they were going to be, and how much fun we and our guests were going to have. Unfortunately, I got about twenty yards down the gravel driveway, applied the front brake too suddenly, and went down hard on my right shoulder. After spending a miserable night, we went to the ER in Monterrey and found that I had shattered my collarbone. The doctor said the best he could do was pain pills and a sling. I asked him how long, and he said, "Oh, about four weeks usually," which was just the right amount of time to ruin our four-week stay. So, pills and a sling it was, which weren't so bad once you got used to them.

Except that it got worse. Usually during the day, we would just relax, pass the time enjoying the view, talking, playing cards, whatever. A few days in, I was indeed relaxing (as best I could with a sore shoulder and a sling) with a book but began to notice a nagging pain in my upper abdomen, kind of behind my sternum. Not really where my collarbone was, but not too far away, so I sloughed it off as pain transference or something. Until it got really bad, and I was writhing around, unable to get comfortable, and in significant pain. So I drank some water, ate some crackers, and even took some antacids. Nothing helped. Eventually, someone said the magic word: heart. It was getting worse, so I was persuaded to get it looked at. I couldn't drive very well by that time, so I got into our rental car, Linda driving, and off we went to the nearest emergency room (or medic of any kind) in Monterrey, about an hour or so away. When we pulled up, I was in a pretty bad state, clutching my chest, so I sagged into a wheelchair and was taken in immediately. Naturally, the staff suspected I was having a coronary, so I got the full attention of the place. They determined fairly quickly that I didn't have a cardiac issue, but I was in distress, so I was admitted. Soon, they found out I had a really bad gallbladder, one that needed taking out. I was scheduled for surgery, and two surgeries later, on successive days, I was relieved of my gallbladder and nearby stuff, including stones. A few days later I was back in Big Sur enjoying the company and the ambiance.

None of this really dampened our fiftieth. Linda and I had a wonderful stay, enjoyed each other, enjoyed a place we both loved, and were able to share it with our family and best friends. We found a way to ship the bikes back to Norfolk (they made it in good condition), gathered up our stuff, and even took a romantic trip on the Wine Train on the way home. That train involves a slow ride through Napa Valley, with stops for tastings at wineries along the way, and a truly gourmet meal served on board. We had a cozy space all our own, and it was the perfect end to our perfect celebration.

One last note on that trip. Not long after we arrived at our ranch house, a little golden retriever appeared. Typical of a golden, he was friendly and sweet, and we wondered where he lived. The lady who was doing our cooking lived nearby, and we learned from her that he belonged to a family who lived on the ranch. They were out of town for the summer, so he was being fed by another neighbor, and we were told he should not be pampered or let into the house, that he was an "outdoor animal" and was "in training." Well, you can imagine how far those instructions got with Linda. His name was Bodie, and Bodie became our beloved mascot and friend. He played with whatever little kids were around, was given treats from the table, and was allowed to sleep in our bed, all of which was concealed from our cook and anyone else who could have ratted us out to the neighbor. The next time we were in Big Sur, we tried to visit with Bodie but were unable to get in contact with his owners. Linda so remembered and loved him that when we got a golden ourselves a couple of years later, she named him . . . you guessed it . . . Bodie.[9] He's here beside me now, and he still awakens in me great memories of that trip—and of Linda.

---

9   See chapter 16.

4 5

Judy

JUDY IS THE YOUNGEST of Linda's sisters. She had another sister and a younger brother, but as far as I could tell, Linda had a closer relationship with Judy than with any of her other siblings. Judy had (and has) what could be described as a colorful life. She was divorced from her high school sweetheart after three kids, became a domestic and international flight attendant, learned to paint beautifully, lived in lots of different places, and eventually married a man she described as the love of her life. Sadly, after a happy decade or so, they went their separate ways.

Judy was (and is) a very sweet, very genuine person, much like her sister. That's the reason, or one of them, why she's included here. She had many different experiences from Linda's, but she was blessed with the same sunny outlook, the same willingness to accept others, and the same innate sense of being honest and doing the right thing. She was (and is) also blessed with Linda's love of sheer fun. An example they loved to retell is of the night she and Linda went out for dinner (and perhaps a few drinks) and found, when they returned to our house, that they had forgotten the key and were locked out. It was late at night, and I was out of town. After considering other options (calling a locksmith, for example, or breaking a window), they concluded that maybe the doggie door in our garage was the best possibility. For those of you not familiar with doggie doors, canines kind of streamline themselves when they go through, so even doors intended for big dogs aren't that big. But desperate people do desperate things, so they decided to try it.

There is some disagreement about what happened next. Linda always claimed that Judy volunteered for duty, while Judy says she was inveigled or coerced (as in "Linda forgot her key and then made *me* crawl in the doggie door"). In any event, Judy *did* crawl in, despite the fact that she was dressed more for dinner than for slithering through doggie doors. Linda never tired of describing how unladylike and comical Judy looked. Wish I had been there.

During Linda's final illness, Judy offered again and again to come to Norfolk to help. It was near the end when I finally accepted her offers. She visited for several days a couple of weeks before Linda died, and I will always be grateful, not just for her help but for the time she and Linda got to spend together.

After Linda died, she visited again to help my sweet daughter-in-law, Sonya, sort through clothes, jewelry, etc., and take care of the other innumerable details. When I had to go to the ER with what appeared to be BP/heart/lung issues, she stuck with me and got me righted from what were probably symptoms of stress.

The next summer, in 2022, was when I took some of Linda's ashes to Big Sur. Judy generously agreed to go with me, and her willingness to do so is what made it possible, or at least bearable, for me. Judy and I got to know each other better during that time and found that we liked each other a lot. In fact, we took another trip to the California coast the next summer. I needed a fellow Dallas Cowboys fan to make my traditional visit to their training camp in Oxnard, and Judy was the only person I knew who would fly coast-to-coast to see the Cowboys hit tackling dummies. We had such a good time and got so cranked up on the Cowboys that when the season started, we arranged to take Judy's son and his wife to a game.

Judy remains a part of my life, both because I like being with her and because she is such a close link to Linda.

4 6

New Year's Eve

OUR HOME IN RICHMOND had a big suite in the basement (there was a door that opened out to a terrace, so technically it was a "walkout basement"), complete with a full bath and woodburning fireplace. I outfitted a nearby closet with upscale sound equipment, built a bar with storage for lots of glassware, etc., and installed a small refrigerator. Normally, it was sort of an extra family room, but on special occasions, it became a true party room.

The tradition of a New Year's Eve party started simply enough. One holiday season not long after we had moved into that house, we realized we had no particular destination for New Year's Eve, so we informally let the word out that New Year's Eve was going to be held at our house. Given the short notice, we weren't sure anyone was going to show up, but a few did. This was the early seventies, which were basically the same as the sixties, so it turned into a rollicking good time. No, there weren't any drugs (we wouldn't have known where to get them), but plenty of music, alcohol, dancing, and general carousing. Everyone told us what a *great* party it was.

The next year we gave more notice and invited more people, and sure enough, the affair's numbers and intensity increased accordingly. I guess we had (somewhat unintentionally) tapped into pent-up demand for New Year's Eve partying, and it grew every year. I'm not sure how many years we had that party, but at its peak, the neighborhood was clogged with parked cars, the revelry had spread to practically every room in the house, and midnight came and went without any noticeable deflation in partying. We made Harvey Wallbangers, went through gallons of a signature cocktail I called a Black Pearl, had napkins custom-printed for the occasion, and often found people we did not know enjoying the night. One year, as the party was finally winding down in the wee hours, one of our guests became very concerned because she couldn't find her husband anywhere. We mounted a search and finally found him asleep (ahem) under a bed. Neither of them was fit to drive, so they spent the night. We enjoyed having them.

All good things must come to an end, and around 1985 we announced that this party would be the last, to everyone's dismay. In an attempt to ease our withdrawal symptoms, for a couple of years we gathered up a few close friends, hired a minibus, and visited other parties, but it was never the same.

But then we decided we needed to experience New Year's Eve in Times Square. We had no idea what this entailed or what arrangements we needed to make; we just packed a bag, got on a train, and got off at Penn Station. We managed to find a hotel and immediately set off for Times Square. Those of you who have been there on December 31 know that things are not that simple. The crowd begins forming very early in the day, there are only certain entry points, and at least in those days, the whole thing was more mayhem than planned event. There were some barriers and some police personnel on foot that tried to keep surges under control, but the only technique that seemed to be effective involved horses. Just when things seemed to be getting out of hand, mounted troops would show up. No one wanted to dispute territory with those 1,500-pound beasts.

We enjoyed the experience enormously. Because we got there "late," we were pretty far away but close enough to see the ball drop. We worked our way out of the melee and got back to our hotel around three in the morning, ready to collapse, but it was not to be. Sometime that night, there had been a murder on the sidewalk outside our hotel. The place was filled with cops, crime scene tape around a big perimeter, and, yes, a chalk outline of a body on the concrete. I don't remember how we got into the hotel; I suppose we showed the cops our key, but in any case, we finally got to bed. You would think maybe we would have been cured of Times Square Fever, but we actually did it again a couple of years later with some friends of ours. Still fun.

4 7

Spice

I HAVE INTENTIONALLY refrained from getting into intimate things. Those are and will remain forever between just Linda and me. That said, I have to include a happening that was vaguely spicy and has become a staple of family lore, told by us and our kids at the drop of a hat.

I have mentioned Sandbridge and that we spent some vacation time there with some close friends and our respective families, at a house sizeable enough to hold all of us. The house we rented on the occasion I am about to describe was maybe a quarter of a mile from the beachfront. We had dinner, then perhaps played a card or board game until the kids were ready for bed. They ranged in age, at that time, from around seven or eight to around fourteen, mixed boys and girls, all good kids. After they had gone off to bed, we adults broke out a little more wine and a little more music, and after a while, we decided what fun it would be to take a walk on the beach. It was a nice night, so we grabbed more wine, probably, and walked down the road to the beachfront. One of the wives was very much into shells and thought there might be different shells visible at night. After we got to the beach, however, we realized that it was a remarkably dark night. At the time, Sandbridge didn't have streetlights; there was a little moon and star light, but not much, so we gave up the shell idea and just enjoyed the wine and the beach.

Maybe enjoyed the wine a little too much, although I don't recall that anyone was really inebriated. Maybe we could have all passed a Breathalyzer test, but maybe not. Anyway, someone—I honestly don't know who—suggested a skinny-dip. It was really dark, no one else was on the beach, and we were all good friends (well, not good enough to have done this sober), so with some hesitation but great hilarity, our clothes fell off. There was a sort of low wall between the road and the beach, so we left our clothes there and trooped down to the water. There was some attempt to cover up, as I recall, but in general it was just a good Bohemian lark, and we were enjoying it.

Until one of us heard what sounded like giggling or rustling up toward the road. We thought, surely, we had been spotted and that the cops were being called, but we soon discovered it was far worse. The kids—all of them—were on or behind that little wall, and yes, our clothes were in their hands, and they were running, on the way to who knows where. Suddenly, we were facing the prospect of doing a perp walk back that quarter mile—naked. This was not something we had bargained for.

One of our number, Harry, either saw or deduced who the lead prankster was and promptly gave chase. Fortunately, he caught him, and our clothes were retrieved. While it was somewhat awkward getting dressed under those circumstances, it was a hell of a lot better than it could have been. Oddly, or maybe not so oddly, none of the kids, even the girls, seemed to be embarrassed or embarrassed for us.

There were two other occasions when Linda and I went skinny-dipping, but those stories are for another day. One family legend of this sort is enough.

48

Valentines and Anniversaries

LINDA AND I were not great letter writers. Even in our courting years, we did more talking on the phone than anything else, and in later years, we used (like everyone else) electronic means to keep in touch. But we did write sometimes, and although sometimes it was just playful, usually if we took the trouble to write, it was from the heart. This remembrance wouldn't be complete without a few of these writings. All of the notes and letters I've included here (unedited) were things one of us saved; I knew I had saved some things I particularly treasured, but I was deeply touched when I found some of our exchanges among Linda's files after she died. I had no idea she had kept them.

Chronologically, the earliest piece is a card, handmade with a piece of folded-over paper, probably because a printed card would have been an extravagance for us in those days. It said, "Happy Six Months' Anniversary, Bill," and had a heart drawn on it with "I Love You!" in the heart. Inside, it said this:

> *The first six months have been so good*
> *And I was very sure they would*
> *As months go by, I love you more*
> *Even though we are so poor!*
> *Love, Linda*

Valentine's Day was a favorite of ours. Linda tended to give me cards; I think she enjoyed looking for one with just the right sentiment. I was more into writing something myself, as in this note:

February 14, 1991

Linda,
I am glad you are with me this Valentine's Day.
I am glad you have been with me for ones gone by.
You have made my life richer: ups, downs and around corners.
And more exciting: your colors are brighter than mine.
Sometimes you have made my life simply bearable; I love you.
We were together in body before we were together in spirit.
But finally, slowly, we found each other.
We each offered parts of ourselves to the other,
Hesitantly sometimes, as if we were afraid our offering might be scorned.
I hope I made you feel I accepted yours.
You always accepted mine, and shared it, and made me glad I brought it.
You need only barely whisper other pieces of yourself to me.
I will listen hard; I will give back the pieces unbroken.
I love you.
You are the center of my life.
Without you nothing else would mean very much.

Another Valentine's Day letter was around the time Linda's hip and back were really beginning to bring her down. I'm not sure whether the following was before or after her big back surgery, but I must have thought she needed a little cheering up, so I gave her this note, on a card that had a painting of a train on the front:

> *Linda,*
>
> *This was the most special card I had. Sorry it's not really a valentine. I love you very much, and we will get you well and feeling better and looking forward to all the good things we have to look forward to. You mean everything to me, and everything that means anything to me has you in it. When I think of something I enjoy, whether it's a season (I like all of them with you) or a place or something we do, you are what makes it special to me. I really meant it when I said nothing would mean very much without you.*
>
> *Bill*

Anniversaries, obviously, were special too. Sometimes we would take a little trip or buy ourselves a present. In 2008, for example, while we were in Jacksonville, we bought a fancy throw, with "Linda and Bill, August 25, 1962" woven into it. Other years were marked just with dinner out or maybe just a day together doing nothing. The one thing we *never* did was miss celebrating one.

Except in 1999. On August 25 of that year, I had to be in Washington, DC, with a client who was being "interviewed" by the SEC concerning an insider trading allegation. The client had been with me a long time, was a good friend as well, and was under threat of actual prison time. To make the timing worse, I was scheduled to teach my class at UVA the next day. Before I left for DC, I left a note for Linda:

> *Linda,*
>
> *This may turn out to be the first anniversary we've been apart, or maybe not. It's hard to tell what will happen in DC. With any kind of luck, we'll get finished before dinner and I can come home. But if I have to go to Charlottesville [from here], I just have to go. George, and my class, are important to me. They aren't more important to me than you are. Nothing*

is more important than that. But I know you'll understand if I have to do it.

Through the ups and downs, I have always loved you. Sometimes with more hurt than joy, sometimes with a feeling so deep I couldn't express it, sometimes with frustration, but I have always loved you. Happy anniversary.

Love,
Bill

HEY—It just struck me that you could come to Charlottesville and go to my class. That way we could have anniversary and class. Think about it.

Apparently, nothing worked out, because I also found, among the things Linda had saved, this document:

Rain Check
Date: August 25, 1999
The Bearer of this Rain Check, or assigns, is entitled to one Anniversary Celebration of a 37th Wedding Anniversary, at a place and time of the Bearer's choosing. It has been issued with regret, and the Issuer hereof declares his love and commitment to the Bearer notwithstanding his inability to meet the actual and original date of such anniversary.
Issuer: William R. Waddell
Bearer: Linda Waddell
This is an Official Rain Check issued by the Rain Check Indemnity and Guaranty Association
Expires: Never

Yeah, it's a little high school, but sometimes we did things like that.

Expressing sentiments in writing didn't come easily to Linda. She was more expressive with a gesture or subtle body language or a quiet few words. So the anniversary notes she *did* write to me are especially precious. Just after her massive back operation, she gave me a card with this on the front: WHAT WOULD I DO WITHOUT YOU? Then she wrote inside:

> *Bill—I don't ever want to find out. I love you very much. You have been so caring and a rock through all my crappy health problems. I'm sorry you had that job but I would not be where I am—hopeful to walk and do some fun things with you. Soon.*
> *Happy Anniversary,*
> *Linda*

Her last anniversary note was especially sweet, although, as I read it now, painful:

> *August 25, 2020*
>
> *Dear Bill,*
>
> *Happy Anniversary. I love you very much and I always will.*
>
> *I hope someday we can return to Big Sur, and maybe take everyone. You are my sunshine.*
>
> *I am sorry for the times I've hurt your feelings. It wasn't "on purpose." I love you and our life together. I feel lucky to be with you, be your wife and share my life with you. Anniversaries remind me of how we started, where we have been, and where we are. I hope we stay here for a long time.*
>
> *Looking forward to more anniversaries, so please take care of yourself.*
> *Love Always,*
> *Linda*

A little more than a month later, she was diagnosed with terminal cancer.

4 9

A Birthday Letter

I WROTE THIS IN 2007. I include it not so much because it was for her birthday but because it is typical of the way I tried to express to her my thoughts about us. There are some minor changes or deletions to protect intimacies or thoughts no one else could understand:

> *Dear Linda:*
>
> *Happy Birthday. I love you. Every time I think about how many years we've been together, I can't believe it, but then I realize how much we've done and it seems like there was hardly time for it.*
>
> *I really remember only the good times, you know. When things are not so good, I don't always think exclusively about the good times, but when I look back, when I have time to think . . . and I think about my life, you are always the main thing in it, the theme that kept me together, and the place I always went when I needed someone. You always have been the main thing in my life, even if I didn't make you feel that way, and I hope you always will be.*
>
> *I look forward to so many things with you: trips and puppies and serious talks and . . . sunsets in Big Sur. Everything I do means more when you're in it.*
>
> *So happy birthday again. We should be happy about how*

far we've come and where we are and what we have ahead. I hope you believe me when I say you are as beautiful and sexy and sweet as you always have been, and that you're smarter, wiser and more of a rock for me now than you have ever been. Because it's all true.

I love you,
Bill

50

Christmas

CHRISTMAS WAS A BIG DEAL for us. Many, perhaps most, couples and families have their own special customs, rituals, and traditions around Christmas. A near-universal one is spending more money than you should, and we were no exception. We certainly spent money we didn't need to. In the early years we were too busy scratching out a living to be very tempted, although we tried, with telephone calls home we couldn't afford, for example, and rich holiday food. Later, though, we lost all restraint, whether with kid toys or presents for each other or gifts for others. Every year we would tell each other we had overdone it, and every following year we would do it again.

But it was always more than that. It was a warm, close, loving time. If the Christmas season happened to fall during a time when there was stress in our relationship, it was put aside, not just in words but in reality. And sometimes the putting aside was a lasting solution. I can remember Christmases that were genuine healing times. In any case, we weren't faced with that stress very often. Mostly, we just enjoyed family and friends, and, most of all, each other.

Sometimes one of us would devise a Big Gift, kept elaborately secret, to be sprung on Christmas morning. I did that with a new car (one that was going to be "Linda's car") a couple of times and more than once unveiled a trip that way. The Big Gift I remember best, though, grew out of a visit to Montana to see my brother. We attended a charity event out there that featured the work of a local artist named Carol Hagen, who painted beautiful wildlife pieces. She was especially noted for her bears. Linda really loved her work, almost (but not quite) talking me into an extravagant bid on one of her paintings.

After we got home, I cooked up a Christmas idea. We had just gotten Teddy, our second Bernese mountain dog. I thought a painting of Teddy by Ms. Hagen would make a fine present, so I contacted her and commissioned a large (24 x 36) acrylic. She sent me pictures as she went along, and the piece was terrific. Now I had to get the thing in hand without Linda knowing. We were having Christmas that year at one of our sons' houses, so I had the painting shipped to him, with instructions to hide it until Christmas morning. At the proper time, we had Linda sit on a sofa directly across from the covered painting, ripped off the shroud, and presented Teddy. Linda loved it, of course, and couldn't get over the time and trouble that had gone into it. She talked about that unveiling for years. The painting still hangs over our fireplace. By the way, Ms. Hagen's works hang in fine galleries and private collections throughout the US and abroad.

The most intimate exchanges, though, were the Christmas letters we wrote to each other. As we reached middle age, after we had been together a good many years, finding something big or special got harder and harder, so instead of stretching to find a bigger diamond, I often wrote her a love letter for Christmas. Here is one of them:

December 25, 2002

Dear Linda:

Since you wouldn't let me buy you anything this year, I thought I would write you a letter again. Some people would think it was funny to type a love letter, but for me a typed letter takes a lot longer than a written one, so I figure it's more personal.

First, you need to know that the chance to know you and

be with you and love you is the greatest blessing of my life. You are everything to me, and without you I would be very little.

This is, believe it or not, our 41st Christmas together, and I have enjoyed every single one. I remember the ones where we had the toothpick tree as our only tree, and the ones when we drove to Kentucky, and the ones where the boys were Santa age. I can't remember what we told them about Santa on Park Avenue, with no chimney, but I'm sure it was a good story, because I can practically see Rob looking at the tree, with big eyes for what Santa brought.

The ones on Fernleigh Drive were undoubtedly the best. Those were the wonderful growing-up years for the boys but they were also the years when you and I found out a lot about who we were and how we felt about each other. Even during hard times, we always had a great Christmas, or at least that's the way I remember it. A lot of our somewhat strange family Christmas traditions started there.

You probably can't imagine how much I enjoyed giving you gifts, like when I would have a new car in the driveway. I was probably clumsy about it sometimes, but I really did enjoy being able to give you material things. If I ever used that in place of giving you other things you needed, I'm truly sorry. I loved you then and I love you now, and it just made me happy to give you things. I remember so well the year on Park Avenue—maybe the first year when we really had extra money—when I gave you several things, including a new vacuum cleaner. When I brought that vacuum in, you started crying and said I was being too good to you. Yes, it was silly to cry over a vacuum cleaner, but being able to buy anything was a kick for us then, and it made me feel good to be able to thrill you with something that mundane.

So I just need to tell you how much you mean to me, especially at this time of year. Christmas is so special with you because it goes with who you are: kind and loving and generous. If ever there was someone who represents the true spirit of the day, the basic goodness, it's you. I feel so lucky to have you, and I don't tell you nearly often enough.

Another thing I don't tell you often enough, by the way, is how much I respect your intuitive understanding of things. You have a great sense of people and events. I'm always amazed at how good your opinions are, and how much I can learn from you. Maybe it's a female thing, but your insights are ever so much better than you think they are.

I hope we can be together forever; that wouldn't be long enough to enjoy your warmth. You are my lover, my psychiatrist, my fun-loving friend and companion, and I just love to be with you. I will always always love you.

Merry Christmas,
Bill

Often, I got a Christmas letter or card in return, like the one with a mushy Emily Matthews poem about A Journey of Love, with this note at the end:

This card says everything better than I can. I just wanted to wish you and us a very happy new year together. We will work out things together (backs, trips, sickness, etc.)!

I really love you and "without you nothing else would mean very much."

Linda

I want to finish this Christmas chapter on a lighter note, and in any case, I can't leave without explaining my reference to "strange family Christmas traditions." Ours were probably no stranger than other families, or maybe they were. One was to go to the all-night drugstore on Christmas Eve. For many years, there was a drugstore in

Richmond that was open twenty-four seven, and late on Christmas Eve, there were lots of last-minute shoppers getting candy or toys or urgently needed replacement bulbs, etc. It was bustling and crowded and famous enough to be covered by the local news once in a while. It became one of our things to do. We always found some musical elf or something to serve as that year's all-night drugstore symbol.

Another tradition was to go to a Chinese restaurant. We had always had dinner at home on Christmas Eve, until one year when, for some reason, we decided to go out to eat. Being inexperienced, we didn't realize, at least when the custom started, that most places closed early. We called around, then rode around (before cell phones or internet), and were on the verge of starvation and frustration when someone spotted a Chinese place that was (logically, when we thought about it) open. We had a great meal, and after that, we always worked a Chinese restaurant into the plan.

One of our traditions resulted in a permanent record of Christmases. We were early adopters of two things technological: computers and video cameras. Our early computer was an Apple II, and I like to think it was a seminal influence on at least one of our sons, who became very accomplished in building software. The early videocam was one of those big boxes that you had to carry on your shoulder, with a heavy cable running to a VHS deck containing one of those big VHS tapes. Clumsy as it was, it all seemed (in fact was) very state-of-the-art at the time. I bought one of the very first available consumer models in the very early 1980s, and from that Christmas until maybe 2005, I recorded every Christmas morning, with each of us presenting and talking about our gifts, what we liked best, etc. It is fascinating now to watch those old tapes, with Linda and me aging and the kids growing up, year by year.

One more tradition: We always tried to find a charitable thing to do. It started when, a few years into our marriage, I realized we actually had some extra money. At the time, one of the local radio stations in Richmond did a Christmas Shoe Fund, which provided shoes to those who couldn't afford them (before the days of Air Jordans and Trump Sneakers). The campaign was headed by a longtime radio personality named Alden Aroe, and on Christmas Eve I was listening when he was on the air with a last-minute appeal. On impulse, I guess, I went to the station late on Christmas Eve and was actually able to talk to Mr. Aroe when he was on a break. I asked what it would take to reach the fund's stated goal. Turned out, it wasn't that much, so I wrote a check. Although I didn't hear it, I'm told he mentioned the incident on the air later.

But perhaps the most memorable gifts were to the Salvation Army. The story behind those is being told here publicly for the first time. Around 1995, there was a spate of news stories about gold coins being found in the Red Kettles of the Salvation Army. Linda and I got the bright idea of donating such a coin since, as far as we knew, there had never been one found in the Norfolk area. Linda was deputed to acquire the coin and found a South African Krugerrand that seemed just right. The actual giving sounds simple, but I started worrying about losing the desired anonymity and about the coin being lost in the shuffle of emptying the kettle. The first worry was easily handled by wrapping the Krugerrand in a dollar bill and having one of my sons (Alex, I think) casually walk by the kettle and make the drop when the bellringer wasn't looking.

The second worry, having the coin overlooked or pilfered, was more challenging. I decided to notify the Army, in advance, that on a certain date, there would be a special gift in the kettle we were planning to use. But I had to do so without revealing my identity. So, late one night, I called from a pay phone (caller ID had just become a thing) and left a message.

We made the drop, thinking that would be the end of it, but it turned out that the Salvation Army thought the event was a good publicity opportunity, called the media, and the next day there was a story in the local paper *and* a blurb on the local TV news (appearing several times). All that would have been fine, except that the blurb included a recording of my phone call. I sounded like a cross between a secret agent and a kidnapper giving instructions for delivering a ransom, about which I got unmercifully teased for years. Fortunately, nobody recognized my voice, and my family was sworn to secrecy, so I didn't get made fun of publicly. The next year we did it again, but with a more skillful cover-up. This part of our giving "tradition" lasted only those two years, but someday I might do it again.

We were lucky enough to have all three of our boys with us on Christmas morning for many years. I'm not positive when that ended, but it was long after we had moved to Norfolk, perhaps 2005 or so. But even after we didn't have all of them, and then, eventually, none of them, Christmas morning was still magic for me and Linda.

51

Not All Roses; Clocks

WELL, NO, IT WASN'T all roses. Reciting the down times is not what this book is about, but I shouldn't leave the impression that ours was a storybook romance without any rough places, because it wasn't. Some rough places were of the garden variety, growing out of different views of something (e.g., how to discipline kids or how many clothes were enough), but the serious ones were about our very relationship, our devotion to each other, our willingness to merge. In the 1970s and into the '80s, there was a concept about relationships that was popular, indeed dogmatic at times, known as "enmeshment." As with many trendy concepts, it had truth in it but was seized upon by some as a sort of universal curative principle for relationships. Everyone, particularly women, was thought to be "enmeshed," in urgent need of self-appreciation, self-assertion, and maybe even extraction from their toxic relationship. As trendy things with a ring of truth tend to do, this had an effect on the prevailing view of relationships, both publicly and in the counseling trade. One of my female friends, a wonderful and intelligent person but somewhat given to the latest trends, explained it to me with a pair of salt-and-pepper shakers, moving them around to indicate that they must not be too close together, and at all costs their contents must not be mixed.

My view was and is that all this is a little unbalanced, and the most loving relationships respect the need for individual self-respect but also involve a measure of things like selflessness and giving in and becoming one. Linda and I struggled with this from time to time, not in these terms, but that was the underlying ground fault, at least as I look back. We always worked our way through, but it wasn't always easy. There was a short time—weeks or a month or two—when we lived separately. We were both miserable and soon realized how desperately we wanted, as the song says, the good times to outweigh the bad.

The reason I mention down times at all is as a prelude to explaining how we crawled out of them. The usual ways, I guess, with "I'm sorry" or "Let's start over" and sometimes with help from wonderful and/or wise people around us. One of those was a man named Dennis Hawley, in Richmond. Our forties (the 1980s) were turbulent for us in some ways, maybe a transition or a shakedown or some restlessness or something. As I say, we actually separated for a while, and Dennis helped us understand what was going on, although it was of course Linda and I who had to do the actual crawling. My part in all this involved, of all things, a clock. In terms of romantic reconciliation, some men would think a poem was the thing, but I wasn't very good at that, so I built a clock. A colonial wall clock, from a kit that required finishing a lot of wood, fitting a lot of clock mechanisms, and getting it all adjusted and running. I had a kind of workshop that Linda walked through every day on the way to her car, so elaborate excuses, lies, and cover-ups were necessary to keep it a surprise. Finally, it was finished, complete with a plate inside the door:

> Linda:
> *You are the center of my life, and without you nothing else would mean very much. I love you.*
> Bill

The lady who did the inscription thought it was really touching and that Linda was really lucky, although I could tell she didn't think a clock was very romantic. But Linda did love receiving that clock, and I think she understood how much love there was in it. We hung it in our dining room. A year or two before Linda's diagnosis, it stopped working. When the dining room became Linda's bedroom, I wanted to get it repaired so we could hear the chimes, but I was told it really couldn't be fixed, that it probably needed a complete new movement, and that the movement would have to be ordered from Germany. I set about searching for such a movement, finally finding one (I think in the Midwest) and getting it overnighted to me. Finding someone willing to install it was equally challenging, but I finally found a guy and took the clock to his house, where his shop was. By this time, Linda was really, *really* sick, and I told him the story and begged him to do it quickly so she could see it. He had it ready the next day, refused to charge me anything, and sent me a heartfelt note of sympathy. Bless him.

I hope our kids love that clock as much as we did and understand how important tangible symbols can be.

Linda and Bill at Her Grandparents' Farm, circa 1962

Linda and Her Beloved Thunderbird

Four Inseparable Friends

Fiftieth Anniversary Celebration HQ, Big Sur

Fiftieth Anniversary Celebration on the Beach, Big Sur

PART VI
The Final Act

I STRUGGLED TO FIND the right word for the title of this last part. It's about the end of something, but I try to think of it as a completion instead of a loss. Linda and I had a life together that was in every way rich and varied and fulfilling and loving, and although those things will fade from memory over time, they will never be entirely lost, or so I choose to believe. On the other hand, Linda was lost to me, finally and irrevocably; I rejected *bittersweet* as a word to describe our parting because it was all bitter and no sweet. So this last part is simply about what went into that pile of conflicts and what it felt like to me.

5 2

Parting

IN ONE SENSE, it was like a thunderbolt, but in another sense, Linda's illness crept up on us, at least looking back. For some years, she had had some breathing problems—shortness of breath or feeling congested—and underwent various scans and other diagnostic imaging, breathing tests, etc., to nail down what was causing it. In 2018 or so, she was formally diagnosed with COPD and began occasionally using an inhaler. It continued to worsen, and in 2020, her pulmonary specialist ordered a biopsy of some suspicious nodes that had appeared in a CT scan of her lungs. When the results came back, we went together to the specialist's office to go over the results. He reviewed the individual biopsies with us, none of which had shown cancer. We were pleased, of course, although neither of us had really been specifically worried about cancer; we had been fighting lung congestion and breathing problems for years, so we just thought the COPD, or whatever, was the problem.

But then Linda's breathing became really bad, and the specialist put her on oxygen. By now I wasn't very happy with the quality of care she was getting from her pulmonary guy, and she eventually agreed, so we arranged to see a different pulmonologist. At about the same time, she began having abdominal pain, so our PCP ordered a new CT scan. The new scan showed nodes that were read as probable cancer but, worse, showed similar nodes nearby in her liver. A PET scan and biopsy confirmed the worst: Stage 4 small-cell lung cancer, metastasized to her liver. By now, we were seeing an oncologist, who told us honestly, although not in so many words, that this was as bad as it gets, in terms of outlook. All this took place over about a month or so, on either side of Linda's eightieth birthday on October 3, 2020. She later referred to it as her birthday present.

Despite the prognosis, we got geared up for the fight. From the beginning, I think Linda was a little more resigned to the inevitable than I was. She said she had lived a great life and that she had always sort of suspected eighty would be her limit. Her attitude was sadness, but with resignation, while mine was more anger and determination. The oncologist was advising that the go-to chemo regimen would almost certainly produce some improvement initially, but then almost as certainly lose its effectiveness. He also described in unvarnished terms the inevitable side effects. How long? He said the average was months, but there was a chance it would be longer.

Looking back, I think treatment of terminal cancer has two equally important purposes: First, it does confront the disease, often having at least a temporary ameliorating and occasionally an almost miraculous long-term effect. But just as importantly, it provides distraction, hope, and a sense of purpose. You don't know if you don't try, and facing squarely the prospect of loss, without distraction and without hope, is too excruciating for most of us to bear. So I think the decision to undergo chemo was the right one, even though it turned out, in the end, not to be even averagely effective for Linda.

I won't recount details of the nightmare that is terminal cancer. However bad you imagine it, from a physical, medical standpoint, it's worse. I will just say this: Linda was as brave, stoic, and uncomplaining as anyone could ever be. This is not to say there weren't rough places in her care from time to time, but she was incredibly brave, far braver than I would have been.

Remember, this was in the very midst of COVID-19. We were

masked, isolated, and doubly fearful that one of us would catch it, a disaster for Linda for obvious reasons and a disaster for me because I wouldn't be able to take care of her. But there wasn't much we could do. We had to venture out for medical care, but otherwise, we just did what everyone else was doing: staying home, going out and letting others in only as necessary, and wearing a mask in public. Thankfully, neither of us was struck, but the restrictions made a bad situation worse. The holidays, Thanksgiving and Christmas, were especially painful because we thought it was too risky to get family together.

For Thanksgiving, our nearby son and daughter-in-law left an entire traditional Thanksgiving dinner on our doorstep. I brought it in, unwrapped it wearing gloves, and set it up in our dining room. We seldom used our "formal dining room," but I decorated it with fall colors and a white tablecloth and our best china and sterling. We set up phones in such a way that we and our son's family could see and hear each other and proceeded to virtually share the turkey dinner they had brought.

Christmas that year was handled sort of the same way. We all sent boxes to one another and opened them on a Zoom call. It was an especially emotional day because we knew in our hearts the unstated truth: This would probably be the last Christmas we would all spend together.

Although COVID began to ease a little as 2020 turned into 2021, the risk to Linda was still extreme. Her lungs were compromised, she was weakened by chemo, and she was on oxygen full time. We discouraged visitors and obviously didn't go out ourselves except for treatments. It added to the sense of isolation and aloneness.

In a perverse way, this semi-isolation brought Linda and me closer. We just had each other. We sat around and watched movies, old and new, watched series we had already seen but wanted to see again (like *The Sopranos*), and just talked. I had just had most of our old video tapes and printed photos digitized, so we looked at those and did a bunch of reminiscing. I got a recliner, in which Linda was much more comfortable. She was on full-time oxygen, requiring a floor model oxygen generator. I rigged up her lines in a way that allowed her to go back and forth to the kitchen or bathroom and fixed an extension so she could have her oxygen upstairs in our bedroom at night.

I did the food prep and cooking and learned a lot about how to minimize the number of times I had to go to the grocery store (buying in bulk, for example) and a lot about what Linda liked to eat and, later, *could* eat. It wasn't fancy or complicated fare. One of the challenges, as she got worse and as the chemo took hold, was to keep her eating and keep her weight up. I developed an ice cream/Ensure milk shake, made in a frozen mug, that was really good and very nutritional; it became an everyday staple. I often told Linda I enjoyed being with her this way. She was concerned that I felt tied down or confined, but I really didn't.

Around the first part of March, Linda had a fall. She got up to use the bathroom in the middle of the night, simply collapsed, and couldn't get up. She was conscious, but woozy, and said she didn't feel right. She didn't admit that easily, so I decided to call 911. The EMTs quickly decided she should go to the hospital. I wasn't sure, of course, whether this was something temporary or something worse. A lot of COVID restrictions were still in place, particularly in the healthcare community, so when I got to the ER, I was told I could not go in. Period. I sat in my car that night for eight hours, waiting. I was able to be in touch with nurses, but the ER rule was unbending: No visitors. I called the boys and told them what was going on and that I didn't know if this was the beginning of the end.

In the morning, Linda was admitted; the hospital docs wanted to do a more complete workup to see just what her condition really was. I was soon able to see her, and I found her in pretty good spirits, all things considered. She was in a semiprivate room, so we didn't have much privacy, but we did the best we could.

After several days of tests and evaluation, including an

independent evaluation of the cancer, the hospital agreed she needed a hospital bed at home and should be close to caregivers. These requirements, along with her now-impaired mobility, all but dictated that she have her bedroom on the ground floor of our house. I sent for help from my son. He rearranged our dining room to accommodate a bed and other necessary items, and we entered the next phase of Linda's care. As I think back on it, this may have been Linda's worst single psychological blow. Her daily existence was disrupted; she couldn't even sleep in her own bed, reminded of her illness at every turn.

After she came home from the hospital, I tried to change the rest of our existing routine as little as possible. She was having trouble walking by then, using a walker to get around, so I would help her get up and into the family room in the morning, where we would typically spend the day, except when she wanted to nap or we had a medical appointment. Lots of ice-cream shakes and old movies and talking and reminiscing. Linda spent a fair amount of time on the phone, too, although she got tired, she said, of telling people how she was.

One of her greatest fears was that she would have to go to a nursing home or some other facility; she asked me several times whether I thought there was any risk of that, and I promised every time that there was no way I would let that happen. Having to live in our dining room, converted to a hospital room, wasn't good, but it wasn't as bad as being in a "facility." I tried to soften the disruption, first by making her new bedroom as friendly as possible and second by sticking to our existing routine as best I could. We gradually learned what needed to be kept near her bed. I initially tried to sleep in her new bedroom, but for a variety of reasons, it didn't work and was of no comfort to Linda. As a partial solution, I got a baby monitor. Each night I would kiss Linda goodnight before I went up to bed, but then I would tell her through the monitor how much I loved her, and we would exchange another goodnight.

From the time Linda was diagnosed, I walked a fine line between dwelling in despair and being unrealistically optimistic. I never tried to convince her that she was just going to get well; I didn't think a big dose of sunshine, followed by a cruel letdown, would be very kind. But I leaned toward hope and confidence; I thought that was the best I could do and might even be an ingredient of recovery. There was one time when I may have leaned too far. In February 2021 scans were showing exactly what was predicted: the tumors were shrinking. When we left the doctor's office, I started crying, hugged Linda, and said, "Honey, for the first time, I really think we're going to beat this." Thank goodness, I don't think Linda bought into it as much as I did.

But my hope was not to live very long. The evaluation that was done in the hospital, and scans soon thereafter, showed the tumors growing again, with fluid beginning to build up in Linda's lungs, eventually requiring a permanent drain. This was not only a turning point from the standpoint of medical outlook, but it marked the point where I could no longer practically do everything needed to take care of her. I engaged a home nursing agency so someone would be there at night, just to watch over her and help her get to the portable commode we had placed in her room. I still kissed her goodnight every night and still told her I loved her on the monitor after I got upstairs.

One of her caregivers, a wonderful woman named Omara, became a real friend, both to Linda and me. She didn't have a bunch of certifications, like some of the other people my agency sent, but we found her smart, knowledgeable about medicine and medical care, and genuinely caring. We made sure she was assigned to us as much as possible, and Linda was always glad to see her, whether it was first thing in the morning or joining in watching some TV show. She helped me with the trip to the beach house for the "girls weekend," which I could not have done without her.

Omara also gave me all sorts of household advice and tips about cleaning, cooking, and organization, small but important things, like how to avoid scratching nonstick pans. Toward the end, she shared her experience about the dying process, something I had never seen or been involved in. Omara and I have been in touch from time to time since Linda's death. Omara, if you read this, I will be eternally grateful for your help, and I wish you well.

It wasn't long after Linda's hospital stay that we had to decide whether to continue chemo. The oncologists had said definitively that the first-line treatment had run its course and would no longer be effective. The immunotherapy we had added was not having any effect either. Different chemo, we were told, was extremely hard on the patient, the chance it would be of even short-term benefit was very small, and the chance of long-term benefit was zero. There were simply no more choices available. Hospice, we were told, was the only alternative that made any sense.

Just the word was a hammer blow. It was giving up, facing the inevitable, and going from hope to bitter acceptance, from living to waiting for death. But it was the right thing to do. Hospice providers are skilled in the art and agony of the end of life and experienced in dealing with it. They are even skilled at preserving what little hope is possible when death is inevitable (not so much through religious belief, although they are very aware of the value of that for believers), pointing out that one can be in hospice for long periods. Jimmy Carter is often cited; he was in hospice for literally years. We were fortunate to have the services of an excellent hospice provider.

I will avoid further details of that period. At some point, I engaged twenty-four-hour care, just so someone would be with Linda all the time. She gradually slipped into a sort of sleep, her pain eased with liquid morphine. I let our sons know the time had come, and they all made it in time to be with her when she finally slipped away. I cannot possibly convey the feeling of that loss. God, or the Universe, or something, provides a stun, shock, or numbness that allows you (or at least allowed me) to survive. Even now, I see those days in a fog. I think I feel the blow harder right now.

53

Memorials

LIFE AND DEATH are mysteries. Each of us attempts to defeat death in our own way. I do not pretend to have any ultimate or eternal insight or answer to the sting of death; I will leave that to others. But I have an abiding belief that at least part of the answer, in a here-and-now sense, lies simply in *remembrance*. Linda will not be entirely gone unless we forget her and forget the goodness and light and love and warmth that she brought, and it is part of my love for her that I do my best not to let that happen.

Linda died on June 6, 2021. COVID was still very much in evidence. A lot of people who died in 2020 and early 2021 simply didn't have services, by reason of prudence or legal restrictions. But by June of 2021, public events were beginning to be held. The boys and I decided we should have a memorial service. A lot of people were asking, and the essence of Linda was people: family, friends, neighbors, and others.

The funeral home we were using didn't really have a place for a memorial service/reception. Linda and I didn't belong to a church, so the venue I chose was one of the fine old houses that had been converted to event space in the downtown Norfolk area. One of my neighbors, Trish Hudson, truly a princess of a person, took charge of details: time, notices, dealing with the venue, food, etc. I will be forever indebted to her. The service was held on June 20, 2021, on a warm, sunny, early summer day that was perfect for Linda. My wonderful daughter-in-law, Sonya, was MC, and the man we sometimes called our fourth son, Jon Baliles, gave a warm, heartfelt eulogy. Her best friend, Marilyn Kern, is a cellist, and she played "Ave Maria" with a keyboard accompaniment. There were videos and photos of Linda, some of her favorite music, and I believe Linda would have thought it was just right.

Linda asked that her remains be cremated and her ashes be cast into the surf at Sandbridge Beach. In June 2022, our family and close friends did just that. Her ashes had been in a sealed wooden urn, and after I cast the ashes, I resealed the urn and threw that in as well. By fate or happenstance, the tides were such that it floated out to sea, and we watched it until it disappeared over the horizon. That was, for me, a profound moment. My thoughts were of loss and finality, and it was an extremely emotional few minutes, then and even now. But it was also a moment of remembrance and love, of wishes carried out, and of the bonds of family and friends.

I reserved a small amount of her ashes and cast them in places she loved: Big Sur, for example. On another trip, I left some at houses where she grew up and where we lived. I still have a small amount, which I will keep as a permanent, tangible reminder.

I've already talked about how much Linda loved dogs. All small creatures, really. So, when I began thinking about a permanent memorial, my thoughts naturally included them. I knew Linda, given her whimsical nature, would have approved.

We lived in Richmond for many years and knew the SPCA there was a great organization. They are especially good at recognizing people who have been friends of the SPCA and animals in general. When one of our very best Richmond friends passed away a few years ago, for example, I (and others) arranged a plaque honoring his support of the SPCA and devotion to animal welfare. So, I contacted them with the idea of creating a space, a place, that would enhance their already-fine facility and be a permanent memorial to Linda. The result is a little park near the SPCA entrance that we named Linda's Garden. A bronze likeness of Linda sits on a bench, holding a small dog, perhaps a puppy, beside her. Two other dogs are standing nearby, their attention on Linda. Her hand is extended toward them, offering a treat. The park signage indicates that it is a tribute to Linda, but its greater purpose is to provide a place to reflect on the extraordinary role animals play in our lives. It has become just that, but also simply a place to sit, and, unexpectedly, a place dogs like to go. We didn't anticipate that, but they seem to regard the bronze canines as kin.

I will share a small ritual that is in the nature of a memorial, something that is private and will last only as long as I do, but it is important to me. Years ago, when we were in Thailand, we admired the "spirit houses" that were everywhere in that country. Many residences seemed to have one, usually mounted on a post or platform of some kind. We were told they were not exactly holy or religious but were consistent with ancient and more modern belief systems that recognize the existence of spirits, including the spirits of ancestors or others who have gone before. They aren't totems and don't have sadness or grief about them, but rather they seem to be about reverence, respect, and a kind of welcoming to whatever spirits need welcoming. Linda and I were taken by the warmth, optimism, and respect for the unknown that these little houses seem to represent.

After we got back from Thailand, Linda ordered a spirit house for me as a Christmas gift. I mounted it on a post in our backyard, facing north as custom demands. After maybe fifteen years, it was pretty deteriorated, so I disposed of it in the recommended way (simply letting it decompose back to the earth) and bought Linda a new one for Christmas. It was more ornate, with dragons symbolizing stability and protection. I mounted it on the same post, facing the same way.

That little spirit house is still there, and every morning we (Bodie and I) go out there and have a little chat with Linda. If there's something weighty on my mind, I may mention it, but usually I just say something about what I did the day before or am going to do that day. And I tell her I miss her and still love her. When I say every day, I mean *every* day, unless I'm not there. Some people would say it's a silly or maudlin thing to do, but to me it's just a little token of remembrance and love, and I intend to do it as long as I'm able.

Finally, of course, this book is essentially a memorial to her. It's a story of love and commitment and the importance of everyday things in a complex relationship, told from the viewpoint of one who appreciates how extraordinary Linda was.

Linda's Garden

5 4

Life Alone

AS I WRITE THIS, Linda has been gone for over four years. Although this book is about us, the two of us, I think I should say a little about my life alone because it probably says something about our life together.

Overarching everything else, there is loneliness. Linda and I were together for sixty-plus years. The sheer separation from her presence is hard to bear. Without regard to any *characteristic* or anything I loved *about* her (and there was more than I can ever describe), just being without someone who has become such an indelible part of your life creates an isolation, a disconnectedness, that is unremitting. Does it fade with time? I suppose so, but in my experience, not very fast. I'm reminded of Wilson, the volleyball, in *Cast Away*. Wilson was Tom Hanks's character's constant, only companion during the years he was stranded on the island. Wilson had no personality, no life, no characteristic to love, but Wilson was *there*, ever-present in Hanks's miserable existence. In the heartbreaking scene where Hanks loses Wilson to the sea, he is utterly devastated. Not because of anything *about* Wilson, but because it rips away something that had become a part of him. So it is with Linda. Obviously, it isn't the *only* way I experience her loss; I'll try to describe some of the other streams of grief around losing her. But even aside from those other streams, the loss of her very presence is painful.

I have come to think of my grief as different streams. The "stages" often used to describe grief may be useful to some, but if anything helps me deal with the loss, it is understanding *types* of grief, where it comes from. One stream arises from the loss of Linda's wisdom. We were different in how we thought things through. I am analytical, while she was much more instinctive, able to grasp the essence of a problem, react to it and evaluate it, without necessarily being able to articulate how she arrived at her conclusion. Over time, I came to respect the validity of her conclusions simply because they often proved themselves right. Analysts are always skeptical of nonanalytic thinking at first, but I became convinced that Linda should be listened to. So I miss her counsel and the way we bounced ideas off each other. Without her, I'm not as smart as I used to be.

Then there is the loss of love, in both directions. Linda's love was warming and buoying, but it was equally satisfying to love her back. It made me happy, made me fulfilled, to love her and let her see my love. Made me happy, I guess, to be able to give her that, and I miss it.

A subset of the loss of love is physical loss. Not necessarily sexual in an overt sense but touches and kisses and playful bumps and the rest. These are uniquely hard to replace. One can at least pretend to cope with mental or spiritual grief, by dismissal or rational means of one kind or another, but there's no replacing, placing to one side, or finding a way around the absence of a kiss, or at least none that I've found.

Finally, there is the sadness that surrounds what *Linda* has lost. One day she was able to enjoy Bodie, the weather, or friends, and the next day, it was gone. This isn't really my grief, but I find myself saying, "Damn. I wish Linda could see this." She was full of life and given to enjoyment and absorbing sensation, and I mourn for her loss of those things.

So the words I inscribed on that clock turned out to be prophetic. I didn't realize it at the time; it was just a sentiment, sincere but inexperienced. I now realize how much truth was in them: Nothing means much anymore, or at least it is paled and diminished without her. That doesn't keep me from being glad for our life and celebrating it as I am here, but it's a fact, with me every day.

5 5

To Linda

AND NOW IT is time to speak to Linda. Not that the rest of you can't read it; it's just that this chapter is to her directly. Doesn't matter if anyone else appreciates or even understands it. It is for her. I am not a poet, and the words will not be immortal or elegant, but they will be something more: They will be from my heart, and they will be true.

Linda,

You are beautiful. In a stunning, corporeal way, of course. But in two other, rarer senses: First, your aura is beautiful. Some people claim to be able to see auras; I can't, but if I could, I'll bet yours would be really warm, indigo or pink or something, because the traits that are supposed to go with those colors (as I understand it) are so completely you—benevolent, giving, compassionate, unselfish. Maybe the most genuine person I've ever known. People, whether they realize it or not, just feel immediately drawn to and comfortable around you.

Second, and maybe more important, you are beautiful in a kind of moral sense. If in the grand scheme of things there is one overarching morality, it has to be the golden rule: From Buddhists to Zoroastrians, through thousands of years, this principle (not always lived by, of course) has underpinned the best of human virtue. You are the very embodiment of it, in your kindness, generosity, and the two sides of the coin of selflessness and unselfishness. It is not in your nature to look at and admire yourself, as the self-esteem mods would have it, so you probably never saw yourself as a great moral example. But you are, and I love you for it.

When we were young, I loved you as young men love young women: passionately and sensually. I dimly recognized even then the generosity and goodness that you were, but I was not nearly wise enough to honor it the way I should have, let alone appreciate the gift that had been given to me, for truly you are a gift. When we were older, I loved you with a fuller realization, a fuller awareness, of who you were and how I loved that *who* and a dawning understanding of what love is, how deeply the tie between two people can run, fragile as it is. Now that we are old (there is no other word for it), I realize, perhaps for the first time fully, how precious and transient life and love are, how desperately I want to absorb your love and have you absorb mine.

Linda, you are truly the center of my life. I love all that you have been to me—and I will always love you. Nothing will take you from me, even if you are not here. We are woven as one. When God, or the Universe, bears you away from me, or bears me away from you, our spirits will be somewhere together. We are woven as one. And if God, or the Universe, should recreate or renew or extend what we know as our lives, we will find each other—because we are woven as one. I love you.

The End

Acknowledgments

I AM GRATEFUL to the many people who helped me tell this story. As I said in the prologue, it began as some random scratchings. Only later did it become a recounting of the warp and woof of the relationship Linda and I had, and only through the generosity of these helping hands:

Jenny Pfeiffer, my life coach and friend, helped me understand my grief and my new life and patiently read and improved *Woven as One*.

Sonya Ravindranath Waddell, my amazing daughter-in-law, assisted me both in the development and editing process.

Miranda Dillon, my editor, Danielle Koehler, my designer, and everyone else at Koehler Books, thank you for a thoroughly professional and friendly operation.

Lauren Hathaway, my publicist, without whose combination of discipline, tolerance for a first-time memoirist, and respect for creativity, I would not have known how to make a readable product or how to help readers find it.

My friend "Amy," read my manuscript and offered, as always, great insight and ideas.

Linda's sweet sister, Judy Curran, was kind enough to read early versions of my book and give me her thoughts, and we shared many a memory of Linda.

And finally, my erstwhile law partner, friend, and well-published author, Gilbert "Bud" Schill, was so vitally helpful at every step, both with the fundamentals, style, and nuances of writing, and with the mysteries of the business side of being published.

Thanks to all.

www.ingramcontent.com/pod-product-compliance
Lightning Source LLC
LaVergne TN
LVHW091542070526
838199LV00002B/168